MW01356765

Freedom | Saoirse

Print ISBN: 978-1-09838-581-1
eBook ISBN: 978-1-09838-582-8

Printed in the United States of America

FREEDOM

Saoírse

Concepta McNamara

TABLE OF CONTENTS

For Patrick (Mack)
and Mary McNamara

FOREWORD

When I first met Concepta, I learned she had kept thick journals of written entries from a many-years-long odyssey. Its origins were in abuse, with subsequent addictions and personal struggles peppering her journey.

When she told me about all of this, I thought, "Here is a story that ought to be told." And with that, we set about trying to make sense of all the journal entries, many of which were terribly misspelled, not chronologically ordered, or just plain unreadable. The analogy I use is that it was like having a seventy-thousand-piece puzzle dumped on our laps, each piece translucent, and no picture to reference on the box.

We developed a process where we'd cobble a few lines and paragraphs together and then I would read them aloud to Concepta, and she'd add some thoughts or edit on the fly. That was our process for more than two years and this book is the result.

It is a story that needed to be told, not so much as a catharsis for her, but as a symbol of resilience in the face of an undeserved, unmitigated robbery of a little girl's innocence. It was that heinous monstrosity and the deeply buried pain from it, that led to addictions, additional abuse, and dissociations from herself and others. She overcame these effects through sheer Irish stubbornness, and with vital help from some incredibly skilled psychotherapists and energy healers.

FREEDOM | *Saoirse* isn't just a memoir. It is a great achievement.

I can think of no one more deserving of that than Concepta McNamara.

Steve DeWaters

Consultant | Writer | Editor.

PROLOGUE

"Hello, my name is Concepta and I am an alcoholic."

That was the opening line of my recovery after joining "The Program" in Alcoholics Anonymous (AA). I learned many things in AA, including statements like this one: *We are only as sick as our secrets.*

Another was that it takes five years of continuous sobriety to get your marbles back and ten years to learn how to play with them.

I lit a cigarette at the age of twelve and swallowed my first drink at the age of fourteen. These were my alternatives to understanding a deeply held, misunderstood pain. By the age of twenty-two, my smoking and drinking were fuses attached to an internal explosive, ready to blow me up with the least wayward spark.

It was then that I was guided toward a path where I began a grueling, slow, dark, and often turbulent process of unraveling the secrets, confusion, and pain that I had carried with me since my early childhood.

Through it all, I also carried fond memories of my tiny fist nestled safely in the hollow of my daddy's hand, as we slowly walked together near our home, just the two of us, father and daughter, a daddy with his innocent little girl, saying things to each other that only he and I could ever know.

He never knew, though, that his daughter's innocence had already been robbed.

° ° °

"He's just messing with you."

That's what my mother told me each time her brother—my uncle—would make me feel uncomfortable.

As a child, I didn't have a name for it, nor did I fully understand the impact his type of attention would have on my life. Over time what I learned from the encounters defined who I was and what I believed affection looked like.

Growing up in an Irish family, with a mother too busy to give me the attention I craved, the only affection I received was from my uncle.

° ° °

While some of the names in the pages that follow have been changed, the abusers were all too real in their complicity and in the shaping of my early life. Even those who are now dead.

Should any of them who are yet still alive ever read this book, my hope is that they can accept the truth of their deviancy. More so, I hope that they can accept my compassion for them.

It is in forgiveness that all true power resides, and I forgive them one and all.

To those who are drawn to this book, I want you to know that whatever trauma you, or someone you know, may have been through in life, it is absolutely possible—with the right kind of therapy and energy healing—to become the person God intended you to be.

The challenges we endure growing up, and the lessons we learn from them, however bizarre or hurtful, can one day benefit other people.

Despite how broken you think you are, it is in the shifting of your thoughts, and reclaiming ownership of your body, that leads to Freedom | *Saoirse.*

Concepta

GALWAY GIRL

It's amazing how some memories stay with you forever.

Not the vignettes that roll through your mind, but the sensory experiences, the memories that come to you as immediately and as real as if they were happening to you in the present moment.

Like the bewitching, earthy aroma of ancient moss—which the Irish call turf—burning in the hearth, or the clinking of Mammy's knitting needles working at another Aran sweater, or the warmth of Daddy's hand curled around my little fist as we walked together along the *boreen* beside our home.

There are so many memories, of the mind and of the body, that it's hard to know where to begin. Scanning through my decades-long collection of journal entries, I can reflect on a hundred moments. Picking one at random to start my story doesn't seem the right approach. So, I will start on the west coast of Ireland, in Galway, where I was born.

Galway is a much smaller city than its more famous eastern cousin, Dublin. Smaller still is Park Corrandulla, the town I grew up in, where there were more cows than people back then.

Smaller yet was the thatched-roof home where we all lived: Mammy, Daddy, my three older brothers, an older sister, and me. There, we used an ass-and-cart to bring sticks and turf home for the fireplace to keep us warm. At home, the roof leaked, there was no indoor plumbing, and many other amenities were missing.

It was also a place where emotional closeness and affections were absent, in a home reminiscent of a monastery, with more silence than dialogue.

° ° °

I slept for the first twelve years of my life between Mammy's cold arse and the cold stone wall of the bedroom. Daddy slept on the outside of the full-size bed.

When I was quite young, I would crawl out of the pram and into my parents' bed, snuggling between them and pushing Daddy to the very edge of the bed, "as quiet as a '*mousheen*,'' he'd say.

When I was a little older, I was shifted to sleeping between Mammy's arse and the wall. On nights I couldn't sleep, I would silently scrape the pink, patterned wallpaper off with my bitten nails. I was always careful to scrape low enough where nobody would see the marks. It was soothing, and it helped me drift off to sleep each night, but I also didn't want to get in trouble for ruining the wallpaper.

Sharing a bed with my parents didn't come from a fear of being alone. It was because there simply were not enough bedrooms or beds.

My mom's feet were always cold, and Daddy would often say, "Take them cold feet away from me." I would chuckle in silence each night he would say it, but she knew they would get warm against his body.

I had a glass bottle of hot water placed in a sock against me to keep me warm. As the night progressed, the bottle would come out of the sock so it would keep me warm for another hour or two. It would get refilled each night, using the back of a spoon, inserted handle-first into the bottle as a channel for the boiling water to flow, preventing the bottle from shattering as the hot water hit the cool glass. Until one day when it shattered anyway.

Daddy's wheezing was a familiar sound, and I would drift off to sleep with it each night. His asthma was with him for many years.

Mammy was often up before Daddy. He was always lovely and warm to snuggle next to. "What are you still doing here?" he'd say to me with a smile, knowing full well I didn't want to get out of bed, to step onto the cold concrete floor to start my day.

The Sacred Heart light was always on in the main room, where we ate and hung out, where we kept the bag of flour that sat on the hob, where a clothesline was strung across the ceiling, and the Saint Brigid's crosses were nailed to the rafters. The one and only electrical outlet in the house was for the wireless.

My dad would often stand next to that wireless placed at the perfect height—ear level—and listen to the *Kennedys* and the *Riordans*, his favorite talk shows on the radio. We were expected to be quiet during this hour.

I was eight when the "television man" came to our house one evening, telling us he had a television for us. We had no idea why. He could have been at the wrong house, but we accepted it anyway, and told him where to set it up, near the solitary outlet, of course. Paddy Ford was his name, but to us he was "the television man."

We were glued to the black-and-white picture on the screen from the moment it "opened" around 2 or 3 in the afternoon until the programming, limited to two channels (RTE 1 and RTE 2), ended around 10 p.m. *How Green Was My Valley,* was the first movie we ever watched, and the first commercial we saw was for orange Fanta. Back then, remote controls didn't exist and that meant there was the novelty of changing the channel and volume manually. We were often reminded by Daddy, "Don't break it."

Eventually, when the TV came with remotes, my dad never could fully enjoy them. Even when we finally got one, he'd leave it next to the TV, walk over to it to change the channel, and then leave the control next to the television again. We never lost it, that's for sure.

"Squitch that off," Daddy often said if there was some program on that didn't interest him, or especially if we had visitors, even if they were a "Tinker." "Tinkers" were people living in a roadside caravan culture, thought to be poor and "lesser than." Even they got his respect and full attention. It was a lesson I continue to carry with me today: giving the people in front of me my full attention.

Occasionally, we'd watch a band of musicians singing on stage, and I can still hear my dad say, "Why are them lads jumping around like that? They must be cracked in the head!"

My dad got a lot of daily exercise from the hard work he did on the farm. He wouldn't know what a "workout" was. He never set foot inside a gym in his entire ninety-two years.

His day would always start with a mug of tea and he'd clean off the right end-corner of the table, a table he made himself. The tea was often accompanied by a cut or two of homemade bread and butter. Sometimes an egg would sit in an eggcup waiting to be cracked open. He would only eat an egg from his own chickens. He never ate a bought egg in his life.

His sleeves were always rolled up on his shirt and he never wore anything but a dress shirt on top of an inside shirt. On cold days he would wear a cardigan with pockets over the shirt. He didn't see the use of a cardigan without pockets because he never went anywhere without the inhaler for his asthma and that fit perfectly in a cardigan pocket.

○ ○ ○

My parents' journey began in the mid-1930s. They knew each other growing up and they were fourth cousins. My dad remembered carrying my mom on top of the handlebars of his High Nelly bike for fun rides. She would have been five or six years old then, and at the time, he was twenty-two.

They never dated. They were "match-made." My dad's sister, Mary, asked my mom if she would marry Patrick Mack when she was twenty-six. My dad was seventeen years older. I don't think she answered straightaway.

The story goes that my mother called her sister, who had emigrated to Boston a few years earlier, and asked her if she should marry Patrick Mack. My aunt must have said yes.

On February 9, 1959, they were wed, and the shindig was held in the old house, built in 1840, a thatched-roof home that was gifted to my dad after his mother died.

Daddy and Mammy, February 9, 1959

Back then, new brides were not allowed to go back home (to their mom's and dad's) for the first month. I'm not sure if that was a tradition, or a way to force the newlyweds to work through any early issues that may have come up in the first month. They had a simple life, a few acres of land, and a small farm with cows, hens, chickens, and an ass or two.

∘ ∘ ∘

Our prayers were always said in the morning or at night, but it would take many years before I knew that I could ask for help or guidance from God 24/7 and not just during the designated time when we said the Rosary. That is how I start most days even now. I ask God, "Do this day with me! Use me!"

Some areas of the floor in the bedroom may have had pieces of Lino, but the main room had concrete; it was impossible to feel warm on it.

The fire was always raked at night so it would still be smoldering most mornings and easier to restart. Some days our clothes would be hanging on the back of chairs close to the fire, getting warm.

I don't remember anyone making me a school lunch, but often I would have a penny biscuit for a treat. Michael O'Fahy was the big lad who would sell them to me for one penny each. Eventually it went up to two pennies, changing them from one-penny biscuits to two-penny biscuits. I still remember the taste of them, dry as dust, but I loved them back then anyway. They didn't have a wrapper and often Michael 'O' would hand them to me. God knows where his hands had been or when they ever got washed.

I remember feeling comfortable for the most part in school. I carried my books and many secrets with me throughout each day. Any time the school principal, Mrs. Henley, was upset with me, for just about any reason—talking to a classmate, not paying attention—she'd knock me on the back of my head with her swollen knuckle, or sometimes she'd tell me to hold out my hand, palm up, and she'd give a slap with a twelve-inch wooden ruler across the top of it. I can still remember the sting of that.

Years later, I developed compassion for her after I found out she lived with a very sick, active alcoholic. She was kinder to her own kids and sent them to a boarding school, away from what I believed was abuse and violence.

I would describe myself as a hermit who liked people, but I rarely remember connecting with anyone, or showing any affection, except when there was thunder and lightning in sixth class. The younger girls feared the lightning. I was afraid also, but the others were even more frightened. I remember staying close to them, hugging some if they needed it, and I told them God was taking pictures and moving furniture. I felt like a mother hen with her young.

Years later, I had a very enlightening chat with a great gal who went to the same school as me. Her perception of me was so different than my own. I liked her version much better. She remembered me as being kind, caring, and thoughtful.

A few memories she shared will always stay with me, including the day her best friend was out sick and she said I made sure to keep an eye on her and asked her if she was OK. I even included her during our lunch break in the school yard.

I am partly that person today, or maybe I always was. I couldn't feel it back then because my internal wiring was crossed, and I carried a secret heaviness within me.

My external life was very simple. I got up each morning, went to school, came home, played outside or down at Clonboo Castle (a four-story fifteenth-century tower house ruin), ate spuds and onions for dinner, went to bed, and started all over again the next day.

Clonboo Castle, where I played as a child

o o o

Mattie Glynn's blue van, with two doors that swung open in the back, was converted into a travelling shop. It lacked the aroma of fresh food like the smell of fresh bread in a bakery, or the scent of a butcher shop. Everything inside the van was wrapped and sealed tightly to keep things from the mold and rot.

It was built with shelving inside it, and he sold the wrapped food as a cash business. He used a pen and paper to keep track. As each item got passed to us, he would write down the amount. "Draw the stroke" was the cue to know that was all we wanted today: draw the stroke and add it up.

A van very like Mattie Glynn's. His was blue.

Mattie was what you would call harmless, never married, always seemed happy and jovial, which are great traits to have in his business. Not everybody shopped at his van, but we did for many years and he would always seem to come around at the same time *Flash Gordon* was on television.

I remember being torn between watching *Flash Gordon* and hoping to get something nice from him, like biscuits or sweets, but mostly it was the basics: flour, sugar, salt. I think he even carried rashers and sausages. We had our own eggs and most of our own vegetables.

Mattie Glynn would sit on a stool in the back of his van, which was small enough that he could reach the items we wanted to buy without getting up. When he stood, he had to bend over.

In addition to the travelling shop, we had a "gas man." He sold barrels of gas that most homes would use for their gas cookers in addition to the open fires.

Mattie's two competitors were Hughes' Shop, a home converted into a makeshift grocery store; and Regan's Pub, where the family lived upstairs from the pub, lounge, and grocery shop.

As more grocery stores developed and became popular, there was less demand for Mattie Glynn's business, and he retired his travelling shop. But he didn't become a stranger.

After he retired the van, his unannounced visits were always welcome. If he had the big bags of flour with him, we'd always buy one. Bags that size could not be gotten at Hughe's or Regan's.

The kettle would always be put on for a cuppa tea, but he'd stay longer when the dust was wiped off the stronger stuff that sat on the top shelf in the "press" (the cabinet, as it's called in America) next to the biscuits.

When I was little, biscuits were my escape. My internal life was confused, and I collected a lot of false information, information that I would later need to unlearn. Survival skills, like comfort through biscuits, came in handy.

We would often wake up to a puddle of water near the back door. The carpet or Lino were never destroyed, as there were none, but you could see traces of the "rain down" on the wallpapered walls, and the stains matched the stained lace curtains. With a concrete floor, it just needed to be mopped up and left to dry naturally.

When the lashing rains came into the house through the thatched roof, pots and saucepans would be left under the drips and emptied when full, which was a round-the-clock job at times.

A bed pan was set under each bed as we didn't have indoor plumbing, and orange peels were often thrown under the bed to mask the smell. We had no idea how poor we were or what it was like to live in a warm home with basics like indoor plumbing. My dad lived this way his entire life, in this same house, and never complained about what he didn't have.

The concrete floor got washed periodically, mostly by my brother Johnny and me. We would get fresh water from the well, usually in the middle of the night when everyone was sleeping. We'd boil the water in the kettle that hung on the hook over the open fire, and we'd scrub the floor with a yard brush. It took many hours to dry.

No matter how often we swept the floor, we would always find a pile of dust that got swept into the ash-hole. This was the hole under the fire. It was also where we found the ashes to rake the fire every night.

Without indoor plumbing, a shower was unheard of, but our hair still needed to be washed. So, growing up I felt like I was drowning every week. One of my parents would pin me down over a plastic basin, while water was poured over my head, soap in my eyes, and the water went into every orifice on my head.

Ears, mouth, eyes, nose all doused in water, my screams got louder, and the process always took what seemed like forever. The panic I experienced, and my hyperventilating, didn't seem to register with either parent. To this day I'm still averse to water and never learned to swim.

When we did get a bath, it meant two chairs being pulled close enough together that they were sturdy, to hold the weight of a galvanized bathtub. It held twenty gallons of water, made warm with a kettle on the fire, and each child was washed in sequence. I always quietly hoped I was the first so I could have the cleanest water. "The Towel" hung on the back of one of the chairs.

A running joke today is, "Where's the Towel?" There was only one towel between all of us. The same towel that wiped my brother's arse, wiped my sister's face. It was a dark towel, so thankfully you couldn't see the dirt. I can still feel its scratchy wetness, and thankfully I have no memory of how it smelled.

For as long as I can remember, I have always been able to see the good in things and I don't have to guess how this was developed. Any complaint as a child was quickly turned around to feeling grateful.

One lesson I recall is when I went to my mom one day complaining about the holes I had in my shoes. I was quickly reminded, "Your father had no shoes at your age," and I learned to feel grateful in that moment. I also learned how to make paper insoles for the shoes that had holes in the bottom of them.

With a Biro (or pencil), we would trace our feet on thick cardboard from an empty box. Then we'd cut around the line with scissors and place the cardboard insoles into our shoes. This would last on dry roads for days, but Ireland didn't see many consecutive dry days, so the cardboard needed to be replaced often.

I loved the black clogs I got when I was eight or nine and still loved them at ten and eleven, until my big toe starting protruding through the front. It didn't matter too much that my foot had grown and my heel was sticking out the back of them. They remained my favorites until my heels were close to an inch over the back of the shoes, and I eventually had to toss them.

I vividly remember certain sounds growing up. One of those sounds is the ticking of the clock that hung on the wall of the room where we all gathered. It needed to be wound weekly through holes on each side of the numbers.

On the weekends especially, I remember my dad stirring his mug of tea, making sure every grain of sugar was melted, and he would stir for what sometimes felt like a ten-minute process, the spoon clinking the cup as he worked. He loved his "bloggum" of tea and his sips and slurps were loud after the stirring.

The days of working at the bog to cut turf always included a bottle of tea and a few cuts of bread for us. We'd all be cutting or turning or stacking the turf, and the break between all the work would feel like a four-course meal. We welcomed and appreciated every mouthful. Most of the time, the tea was kept in the same glass bottle that kept me warm at night in bed. That too would have a sock around it to keep the tea warm.

Then we'd load the ass-and-cart with turf and make the long walk home, where we'd unload and stack the turf to use when we needed it.

Daddy and the ass-and-cart. The cart he made himself.

We kept a galvanized bucket filled with well water on a wooden table behind a door. That was where we kept the butter to keep it cold, because we had no refrigerator.

There was also a green dresser that had a rubbish drawer. It was not that big, but everything seemed to end up in the rubbish drawer. We kept porridge in that green dresser also, along with dishes and other food products. Corn Flakes became a staple.

Often, we were given "goody", a concoction of homemade brown bread, sugar, and tea, served in a mug. "Mush" might be a more apt description and considered a treat in some Irish households. For us, it was often the whole meal, and I think I would have difficulty trying it again today.

The white-washed stone walls and the thatched roof of our home were built in 1840. The stone arch over the main fireplace had that same year carved into it.

The stone arch and fireplace of our home.
Three generations are represented in this picture: my brother Gerry on my mom's lap, my dad, and his father, Ned.

It was the home that my dad was left, as he was the oldest son. It was a tradition in Ireland back then that the oldest son inherited the home and land. He was born and lived there his entire life and he was happy to stay there.

The wooden chair beside the fireplace was quite uncomfortable and the stone hobs were even harder. A thin cushion would get passed back and forth to make the seat more comfortable.

I have many memories of fighting for the warm hob, the empty one that is, because the other one (on the left) was where the big canvas bag of white flour sat to stay dry. It was the only warm spot in the house. The fire was always going, all day every day, and then it would be raked at night.

This was also where Santa Claus delivered some of his presents in different years. Santa's bag was white or pale grey before it made its way down the dirty chimney, and the soot got attached to it when it made its way down.

We had a small amount of land to go with it. Eleven acres is the number I have heard over the years, mostly tillage land, good for farming, but no road frontage and generally it was too wet to have buildings on it.

The thatched-roof house I grew up in

The front door was always unlocked, leading into the main room, the room where we all congregated. In fact, I don't believe it even had a keyhole to lock it from the outside. There was a latch inside that we could lock at night.

There were four rooms off the main room. One was the back hall, which was like being outside. It had a big sink, but with no indoor plumbing, it was useless.

The three other rooms were bedrooms. One had a fireplace with a mantel piece and two beds. Another room had a twin bed, and a full-size bed was in the other.

One brother had a room to himself. I shared a room with my parents, and my sister was also there a lot of the time. The other rooms were for two older brothers and my sister sometimes shared those, as well. The headboards were made of iron and the mattress in the small bed looked more like a hammock, sunken in the middle.

There was a Sacred Heart light attached to a picture of Holy God. Most every Catholic home in Ireland had a picture of Holy God framed on the wall. We also had a water font near the front door. Most of the time it had Holy water in it.

At seven o'clock every night, we'd kneel and say the Rosary shortly after the Angelus, which was at six o'clock. The television or the radio would sound-off the Angelus with twelve recorded tolls from St. Mary's Pro-Cathedral bell. The blessed candles were kept somewhere safe next to the Holy water.

We didn't know what a checkbook or credit card was. We only had Irish pounds and often Daddy would call the coins "a few bob." Every transaction was either cash-based or bartered.

It was a simple life in a simple time, made less complicated by the complete lack of anything technological. Even the telephone would not arrive in my parents' home until five years after I'd left for America.

○ ○ ○

My oldest sister, Mary Theresa, was only a few months old when she died from pneumonia. I have clear childhood memories of wishing I were her, wishing I weren't living, but never expressing that to anyone. I knew no one was there for me, to understand me or my sadness and repressed anger. It was years into my recovery that I would call this "depression."

I can't even begin to imagine what it was like for my parents to lose a child, the first girl after three boys. It was another three years to the month after Mary Theresa's death, when my mom conceived my still-living sister, Noreen, but there may have been at least one miscarriage during that time period also.

The story about my sister, Mary Theresa, was that the doctor had come to our house, which was common practice back then in Ireland. The doctor examined her and said she was OK, but a seasoned neighbor visited moments after the doctor had left to tell my mom that she was *not* well and suggested she be taken to the hospital. The neighbor saw that she had pneumonia, the sweats after bottle feeds being one of the signs.

They took Mary Theresa to the regional hospital. It was a rainy day. My mom's memory of the story was that she handed her child to a nurse at the hospital door, and since she wasn't allowed in to stay with her daughter, she went home to parent my three brothers.

The following day, my dad cycled to the local post office where they had a telephone, the only phone at that time in the village, to call the hospital to see how my sister was doing. That's when he found out his little girl was no longer with us. I'm sure his bike ride home was daunting. He walked through the door and told my mom, "She's in no more pain."

Speaking the words "She died" was too much for him.

I can't imagine that moment, or the days, weeks, months, and years to follow, living with that hole, that space only Mary Theresa could fill.

My sister, Noreen, told me recently that our father, who rarely talked about Mary Theresa, said that months after she'd passed, Mammy got up to make her a bottle after she thought she heard her daughter crying.

Mary Theresa's soul had returned to Heaven after only five and a half months of life. One day, I may understand why she transitioned after such a short life.

Listening to spiritual teachers gives me some ease when they talk about people in their "soul form" and how we are all here for a purpose.

Some stay longer than others.

° ° °

Five of us remain today: My three brothers and my sister. Each time my mom was asked, "How long are you married, Mary?" she would always ask my oldest brother, Ger, "Ger, when were you born?" and she'd add a year to the number he'd give her, to remember how long she was married.

"Ger" is Gerry, born in 1960. He may have been born a musician since he was drawn to music at a young age. A tin whistle was the first instrument I remember him playing. He later became a poet, singer, and songwriter, and he also plays the keyboards. He's well known and admired at his local church for singing in the choir, as well as at pubs and hotels. He's well known for his creativity when it comes to writing eulogies, as well. One of my favorite tunes, which he performs at weddings and funerals, is called "The Lonesome Boatman." He plays it beautifully on his tin whistle and my mother would often comment, "Ye'd stand in the snow listening to him." Gerry has four beautiful children and lives in Galway.

Johnny, born in 1961, is also an artist and I got to see many of his creative drawings throughout my childhood. He carved the sign that hung outside my parents' house with the words "Castle View", as we could see Clonboo Castle just across the *boreen* from the front door. His creative independence took him to America over thirty years ago, where he continues to thrive in his own business as a plasterer, transforming many homes. I'm the proud owner of one of his sculptures. It's of a naked woman's torso; I hang one of my hats on the stub where the head would have been, and a scarf around her waist. He had two children, Kyle Patrick (RIP), and a daughter, my godchild, a beautiful soul. Johnny still lives in the U.S., in Boston.

○ ○ ○

Kyle Patrick was the first grandchild born into our family, Johnny's firstborn, but God must have needed another angel. His death was from Sudden Infant Death Syndrome (SIDS).

Twelve more grandchildren followed over the years, none ever replacing the precious space that was held for Kyle, who'd also died on my parents' thirtieth wedding anniversary, February 9.

I was living in America when he died, and I still remember making the phone call to my brother Gerry in Ireland about Kyle's death. I didn't want to tell my parents over the phone that their grandchild died. I'm sure they didn't make a big deal of their anniversary, but it would have been heavy news to carry regardless of the day.

My mom had the pleasure of holding Kyle when she visited the U.S. My dad only got to see him through photographs. I never heard how they received the news from my brother, but I'm sure it was devastating, echoing the loss of their beloved first daughter, the sister I never got to know, Mary Theresa.

° ° °

Patsy, born in 1963, also had asthma, like Daddy, and at times it was worse than my own. He moved into Galway City at seventeen years old to embark on his first career as a baker. He became a confectioner and was "rolling in the dough," as we used to say. He even designed and made his own wedding cake. He later entered and settled into the medical devices industry where he is still involved. His wedding was the only one of my siblings' that I attended. It was a memorable day. He has four beautiful children and resides in Galway.

Noreen was born in 1967. "Her Majesty" was one of the many names my mom addressed her by, but I don't think she ever felt like the kind of royalty normally attending that title, either. She gave up her "dummy" (known as a pacifier in America) at the age of three because she was told the neighbor's sow ate it, but she continued drinking from a bottle for another year.

Her creativity is displayed through her work as a hairstylist. Noreen has three sons. Her beloved husband, Robert, was diagnosed at the age of fifty-three with frontal lobe dementia (FLD) and he now resides in the same nursing home where my mom took her last breath. I remain in touch frequently with her.

Me and my siblings. I'm in my brother Gerry's arms.

° ° °

I don't remember my exact age when I had my first drink. I think I was around fourteen, but I remember how amazing I felt after my second vodka. "Vodka and white"—white lemonade. No one knew there was alcohol in it, and I assumed people thought it was just white lemonade.

I was in Regan's of Clonboo, Galway with my good pal, Martina. She was a year older. I remember her asking me, "What's wrong with you?" I laughed hysterically as I told her, "Nothing." I believe her next question was, "What are you drinking?" She clearly knew the effects of this fine spirit that was to become my best friend.

She and I had a great friendship and still do, to this day, but there was a time when booze was more important to me than her or my family.

I considered myself shy prior to a second drink, but not after. My smile lit up a room. I had no problem walking confidently across an empty dance floor to get to the bathroom in the lounge at Regan's Pub. I'd otherwise have avoided the open space and walked around it.

I'm sure there was a legal drinking age at that time, but no one ever paid attention to it. It was also common back then for each person at the table to buy a round of drinks. Miko or Eileen, the pub owners, had no clue the vodka was for me. We always hung out with older friends.

From Regan's, it was not uncommon to hitchhike into town, especially on a fine summer's evening when it was still daylight until 10:30 or 11:00 p.m. My mother always told me when I left home, "Don't go to town tonight, be home at a reasonable time."

I heard these words as I left the house when I didn't have alcohol in me. I never heeded them though, after I had three or four drinks in me. I was not aware at the time that I was no longer in charge of my thinking.

Martina's mother was far more easygoing than mine. Martina could be away from home for a few days without anything being said to her until she finally walked in and her mother would say, "She must be hungry."

I loved her mom and wished mine could be as laid-back. Both our moms are, I'm sure, comparing stories about us today in Heaven and watching over us.

The Holy water was ready, and candles would be lit when I wouldn't come home. We didn't have a phone, which I was glad about as there was no means to call and get yelled at.

○ ○ ○

"Concepta is a pleasure to work with if she would only apply herself." This was a typical note written by my teachers in my high school report cards.

I never liked school. Art class was fun. English was, as well, but only because I had a crush on my teacher, Michael Hannify, until his wife, who was also a teacher, got pregnant. It was a fun crush and I always sat up front, willing to do whatever he needed in the classroom, or especially when he had a message to deliver to another teacher.

I'd take my time walking through the school carrying the note to whomever. I felt like I was his pet. I have no idea if he'd even remember me today, as I was one of many, many students he taught.

My least favorite class was gym. I'd often give my gym teacher, Mr. Roche (nickname "Scratch Balls"), a note that I had written, copying my dad's handwriting: "Concepta is unable to attend gym class due to her asthma."

The forged notes guaranteed that I could be found smoking behind the school or outside a shop nearby. In the shuffle of the students coming and going in the large school, it was easy to sneak out and I was hardly missed.

If I had to choose one word that described my attitude during that time it would be "existed." That's what I was doing: existing, not living. Not loving, just existing.

I remember many times I'd look in the full-length mirror in the school bathroom. I'm sure I'd have been considered vain if anyone had caught me, but I was looking for validation, some proof that I was real, that I was in my own body. Seeing myself in the mirror confirmed that I existed, but as soon as I walked away from my reflection, my confidence would disappear.

Starting at the age of fourteen, the Holiday Inn in Salthill was one of my favorite places. There was a DJ working there who is still a good friend today. You were supposed to be twenty-one to get inside, or look the part, and I always looked more mature than I was.

I recall a day when my oldest brother drove me to school and picked up a co-worker at the same time en route. When I was dropped at the school, his co-worker asked what subject I taught. I was glad I looked more like a teacher than a student.

I felt happy to be seen differently than I felt inside. I was an empty shell. Today, I see it was more that I walked around with many secrets locked and sealed tightly in my mind. Secrets I thought I would take to my grave.

My habit at the Holiday Inn was to get there early enough that they didn't have bouncers at the door yet. Once inside, I'd get to know them so that the next time, I could just walk right by them. It worked every time.

The Holiday Inn became a very comfortable place, a second home, where I would always have a drink in hand and cigarettes on the table.

Once, after I'd just lit a cigarette and I was enjoying my drink, a lad asked me to dance. I agreed and then walked onto the dance floor with my cigarette. He asked me if I was going to smoke or dance. I didn't have to think twice. I walked right off the dance floor and enjoyed my cigarette.

On another weekend date (I guess it was a date, but at the time I didn't know what "date" really meant), we had a few drinks at the local bar and then we went into town to a nightclub. I found the bartender there to be a lot more fun than my date, so at the end of the night the bartender and I went for a walk on the "prom" in Salthill (promenade in America).

The next time I went to the local bar, I ran into that same date and he didn't talk to me. I was oblivious to how my previous behavior had impacted him and thought, "What's his problem?" It was years later that I was able to make the connection between his silence and how my behavior affected him.

A year or two earlier, I'd taken a lift home from a neighbor. He drove into a bog road with no houses or people in sight, a safe place to seduce me. A few minutes into that act, he stopped.

He had a moment of clarity, or remembered his wife and kids, and realized what he was doing was wrong. For years after, I wondered, "Why did he stop? What's wrong with me? Why didn't he like me?" This haunted me for years.

I was already used to being violated, but the abuser usually didn't stop until he was satisfied. Today, I quietly thank that guy for having his moment of clarity.

o o o

For all the anecdotes and reflections about my parents and siblings, our iconic Irish house and my upbringing, and perhaps the nicer sides of my childhood, I yet grew up in a home where nothing was discussed or expressed, where blessed candles were lit during storms, with prayers recited daily. There was very little dialogue and zero intimacy.

I gathered so much useless information from the "emotionally constipated" environment I grew up in and there was no laxative for it back then. It became my "normal." It was normal to not receive affection publicly or privately. It just didn't exist.

Had I a place to go, or someone to go to, where questions could be asked of me, attempts made to reach me, to make me feel like I existed, my journey might have been a lot different.

Instead, it was filled with secrets, shame, and silence. Two words that describe the arc of my experience back then are: seduced and abandoned.

° ° °

No number of showers can wash away the deep stain of being sexually abused.

One of my uncles was my primary abuser. Other abusers would follow later in my life.

I was only a little girl when he would be waiting outside the bathroom door of his house while we were visiting. I used to put toilet paper down in the toilet first so he would not hear me pee. I didn't make the connection to the habit I developed, and I continued putting toilet paper in the toilet years later because I felt the shame of being heard urinating, even in a public bathroom.

I later learned the shame was not from being heard urinating, but what happened after urinating when I was a child. It was a "body memory."

I had associated the act of peeing with the shame of being violated, and for many years I did the same thing in the pubs. I thought of the noise urine made when it hit the water in the toilet, but the shame was much deeper than that.

I had also seen him kiss my sister on her lips when we were young teens. In those moments, I was glad it was her and not me.

° ° °

I am the youngest of six children. Five of us are alive and well today, three still live in Galway, Ireland, and two of us came across the pond to America over thirty years ago.

One brother went to America a year before my own departure. That year before I left for America myself was one of depression, excessive drinking, and a deep sense of loss for my brother who'd already gone "over the pond."

I'd be well into my sobriety before I could express the feelings I carried then.

AMERICA

Despite my depression and sadness, I still had hope because I also felt I was destined to go to America.

After obtaining a passport when I was eighteen, I obtained a six-month visa to America, and planned to stay for one month with an aunt.

One month turned into six months after I got a taste of what it was like to make money in the U.S. I cleaned houses two to three days a week at $10/hour, far better than the babysitting I'd done for a few pounds in Ireland. This gave me the freedom to buy my own cigarettes and drinks. I didn't need to leech off my aunt, and that gave me a sense of independence.

I returned home to Ireland two days before my visa expired. I knew if I overstayed, I wouldn't be able to return to America. I wanted to return more than anything.

When I got back to Ireland, I finished my education and took a job at a hospital that was on strike. Every day, I crossed the picket line amidst the shouts and harangues that I was nothing but a scab for defying the strike.

I so appreciated the mornings my brother would drive me through the gate, with my blue uniform hidden in a bag, so I wouldn't have to hear the anger, and I was grateful for his help. Most mornings though, I walked with my head down and ignored the verbal abuse.

Hitchhiking was also a familiar, safe way to travel back then in Ireland. On the mornings when my brother couldn't drive me, I usually hitched rides to work and often to other places in and around Galway.

Usually, it was safe to hitchhike in Ireland, but there was one incident when a man I'd gotten in the car with, reached across and stroked my knee and thigh, but that was as far as he ever got. He wasn't a total stranger, or at least a few of us knew him. I would see him around town in his red Mini and had accepted a ride with him a few times. In fact, one time he stopped to pick me up and there were already three or four women in the car. Two jumped out and waited for the next car to pick them up, but they didn't seem scared, they just didn't want to stay in his energy.

There was one day when my sister came running home on the verge of crying after getting a ride with someone. My friend Martina and I asked if it was a red Mini. My sister acknowledged that it was. I felt derisive about it at the time, as I had been through so much other abuse already, far more violating than a hand on my knee.

To this day, I don't personally know anyone in Ireland who has been held accountable for taking advantage of another person except some of the Catholic priests. Even the monks seem to have slipped through the cracks, and I'm certain the oddball in the red Mini slipped through, as well.

Though I'd returned home to Ireland, all I could think about was going back to America. I felt mentally and emotionally trapped in Ireland. I was hiding too many secrets inside.

Alcohol seemed to give me a sense of freedom from all of that, but America felt like the only place where everything I'd endured in Ireland could become distant memories.

Little did I know then, it was all coming with me to America anyway.

On September 21, 1987, I was back in Shannon Airport, this time with my good friend Martina. I had another one-year visa in hand and Martina had opted to come with me to America.

Immigration at Logan Airport in Boston made me open my two large suitcases, which held most of my belongings. As the immigration officer combed through them, it became clear he didn't trust that I was only staying for a short vacation, so to ensure that I wouldn't stay longer, he stamped my one-year visa for two weeks only. Martina's visa was also stamped for two weeks.

My brother Johnny picked us up at the airport. As he drove us to his home in Brighton, I swore I'd never drive in America because the highways were so big and intimidating, the steering wheel was on the opposite side of the car, and people drove on the other side of the road, as well.

Fifteen days after arriving at Logan Airport, Martina and I were officially "undocumented aliens," as we'd gone past the two-week stamp. After a few months of staying with my brother, we'd overstayed our welcome with him, as well.

Martina and I lived out of our suitcases and didn't care whose couch we wound up on. We became fixtures at the local Irish pubs. Martina found a job as a babysitter. I also babysat and cared for the elderly. These were common jobs for undocumented aliens. We cashed our checks in the pubs, leaving a tip of gratitude for the bartenders.

Martina's stay was interrupted about a year and a half later. She received a horrific phone call telling her that her twenty-two-year-old brother was killed in a head-on collision with an American who was driving on the wrong side of the road in Galway, Ireland. (RIP Declan).

Despite her undocumented alien status, she was able to leave the U.S. It was only those entering the U.S. from Ireland at that time who needed a valid visa.

Before Martina's trip home, many of our friends found out about her loss. As we were hanging out at a local pub in Brighton, some of them offered her a few dollars. Some had even given money to me, to give to her. I spent it on the drink instead. My alcoholism became very evident during this time, although I wouldn't see this until years later and well into my sobriety.

I went with her to the airport, where we waited in Cloud Nine pub for them to call her flight. I didn't know what to say to her or how to address the sadness she felt about her brother's death. Instead, I was impatiently looking at my watch, wishing she would get on the plane so I could drink.

This was how I treated my best friend. Alcohol had its grip on me.

o o o

On a Wednesday, mid-March, I vaguely remember driving my friend's grey BMW home.

A wet night, too, and I was in and out of consciousness, nearly blacking out as I attempted to stay between the lines on the highway.

I have no idea why he let me drive, but he did. I guess I carried myself well and appeared sober. I also had a difficult night with my breathing. My asthma was active, and I'd forgotten my inhaler. The over-the-counter version I bought at a pharmacy was not helping me breathe any easier, and maybe I had smoked too many cigarettes.

I awoke the next morning alone, hungover, with memory flashes of driving home the night before. I felt empty and yet grateful, knowing I had not been in any condition to drive a 4,000-pound weapon, putting many lives at risk, including my friend's and my own. Somehow, I was guided to safety.

As I walked outside there were large green St. Patrick's Day paper hats on my bushes and I remembered I'd taken the hats from the lobby of a hotel without asking. It was an example of the bad habit I had of taking things when I was under the influence of alcohol.

Most of the time, I didn't remember taking things. One time, I took a large American flag and another time, real horseshoes.

The horseshoes I was able to return. My cousin was with me, playing horseshoes at the home of her friend to whom they belonged. I still have no idea where I took the American flag from, and it hung on my bedroom wall until I moved again. I hoped the owners didn't miss the flag too much. I wouldn't know who to return it to anyway.

Something shifted in me the day I awoke from that dangerous drive home. Something I can't adequately describe. I call it a gift, a gift I have never returned: the gift of sobriety.

I had no idea that morning was to become the beginning of living a sober life. It was not my plan, but clearly a higher power saw it was time and intervened.

As I look back, I believe certain people were placed in my life at that time. They were sober and going to AA meetings on a regular basis.

Tom came into the restaurant I worked-in at the time, for lunch almost every day. He would share stories with me about himself and when he used to drink. I had no idea that he was "planting a seed." He was the one who took me to my first AA meeting.

When he asked me to go, I thought he was just lonely and had no one to go with. He was an older gentleman, and his energy felt safe. It took many weeks before I could see that no one goes to an AA meeting unless they have a problem with their drinking.

He saw the condition I was in each day when I opened the restaurant at 11 a.m.: hungover, stoned, or generally a mess. It was clear to him that my life had become unmanageable. I later learned he already had five years of sobriety under his belt.

Alcohol became my "go-to" place, a "best friend," and it helped me navigate from the ages of fourteen to twenty-two. Looking back, I don't know how I would have survived otherwise. On one hand, it helped me forget the pain of abuse and the feeling of abandonment. On the other, it nearly killed me. It was a double-edged sword.

I had no life skills, no clue how to recognize or interpret emotions, no guidance, no boundaries, and no ability to say "no" or to know that that word was also a full sentence.

God clearly steered me home that dark, wet night. Or it might have been my guardian angels. Maybe they were all there. In any case, getting home safely was a gift from God and I truly believe my death was interrupted by a grace:

By finding sobriety at the age of twenty-two.

ADDICTION

To this day I don't personally know much about "The Troubles" in Ireland but on occasion, RTE1 or RTE2 carried televised stories about the war in Northern Ireland between the Catholics and Protestants.

Many of the stories are probably best forgotten, but I had some roommates from Northern Ireland and after a few drinks they would share stories. Things were so bad growing up there, that more than one roommate spent time in St. Elizabeth's Hospital in Boston, a well-known place to detox or treat mental illness. Two of my roommates were patients there.

One roommate, Danny, told a story I will never forget. It was a story that he often shared at 2 or 3 a.m. after a night at the pub, and each time he shared it he fell into sobbing tears. When he was eight years old, a gun was pointed over his shoulder and his dad was shot dead.

Most other stories, though, were more about being strip-searched at the border between Northern Ireland and the Irish Republic. They were not as horrific as seeing a parent shot dead of front of you.

Another roommate, Kevin, was a painter who always had a ladder sticking a few feet off the back of his pickup truck. On a typical Friday night, he had a few drinks after work, and a few too many this night.

There was a 7-Eleven down the street from us. He must have wanted to get cigarettes on his way home and decided to back into a parking spot in front of the store, a natural thing to do. Except when you forget you have a ladder sticking out six or eight feet further than the truck and it shatters the window of the store.

The female officer that was first on the scene sent him home. "Get out of here," she said. I'm sure his Irish charm had much to do with that. He was lucky that night. I'm sure he was undocumented like the rest of us at the time also. Times were different back in the late eighties and early nineties.

Another memorable night was a typical Saturday night when I came home after drinking most of the evening. It was 1 or 2 a.m., I was just in bed, and two of my roommates had stopped home to get some beer and asked me to join them at a house party.

It didn't matter to any of us that I was already in bed, it was a party and of course I was going. A few miles into the drive, with me closest to the passenger side door of the pickup truck with no seatbelt, we drove around a corner and my door flew open and I was suddenly on the road.

Luckily, there had not been a car behind us as it would have been a much different story. I later learned the driver blessed himself before he jumped out and checked on me to see if I was OK. I was badly bruised but didn't feel much at the time since the alcohol in my system was a buffer. My shoe had fallen off and my friends picked both me and my shoe up, and then we proceeded to the party.

The road rash I had was evident on my leg through the rips and tears in my white cotton pants. It was not until the next morning when my eyes opened, and the booze had worn off, that I found I was unable to move my right hip. It clearly was the side I landed on when I fell.

Having no health insurance and being undocumented, the emergency room was not a place I wanted to go. I was blessed that nothing was broken, and I knew I just needed time and rest. I was unable to work for a few days, but I never blamed the booze. Instead, I thought maybe the truck door was broken or that I didn't close it properly.

I was just grateful that I didn't have to get X-rays or medical attention. My choices didn't lead to good decisions when I'd been drinking. It would take me getting sober to be able to see and admit to this.

Alcohol, marijuana, cocaine. None of those scared me. Prescription meds did.

One indelible memory of being on cocaine, was how quickly I could clean my apartment. Instead of a couple of hours, I could do it in ten or twenty minutes. Also, I would do a few lines at work and when the time came for my shift to end, I didn't want to leave. I had so much energy I'd just want to keep working.

The "speed" energy didn't last long, and the second hit was never as powerful. "Weed," on the other hand, slowed me down, always made me paranoid and hungry. Sometimes I would black out. Today, I think it might often have been laced with something more than marijuana.

I went on many drug-induced trips, mostly alone. The scariest one, that will never leave my memory, was when I was sitting on my floor on a cushion, watching TV. To this day, I have no memory of how many hours and minutes it lasted, but I was in a frightened, hallucinatory state, and it was as clear as watching a movie.

I saw myself being dragged across the hardwood floor and out the door by my hair. I could see a hand wrapped around my hair and I remember reaching for my landline, because I wanted to call a girlfriend I worked with. She was someone I'd gotten high with before, and I asked her to come over because I was scared.

I walked outside waiting for her to come. I was holding onto a post on the deck of my apartment unable to let go.

My friend unwrapped my arms. They were wrapped so tightly around the post that I was unable to walk or feel my body once she pried me away. I remember her calm and smiling face and I think she thought it was funny, but I felt like I was dying and asked her to take me to the hospital. She, and the friends she came with, were scared that the doctors would ask what happened to me, and we were afraid they might make us tell them who had given us the drugs.

I went back inside and sat on the couch. I felt like leaning back, but I also felt if I leaned back all the way, I would die. It was in that moment that my life literally flashed in front of me. It's an expression I'd always heard, but I never experienced it until that night and not ever since, either.

It truly was like watching a movie of my life. Even parts of my life where there had never been a camera to capture the pictures flashing in front of me.

It felt like a near death experience without the white light. I just knew that if I continued leaning back, to feel the back of the chair, it would be over, but a part of me stayed upright with the movie still playing. I became very silent, in a trance, unable to talk, perfectly still. Eventually, I went to bed.

I woke up the next day and bought more weed from the same people who sold it to me the day before. I remember thinking, "I won't smoke as much next time."

They say it's hard to scare an addict, and that's true. An addict in the throes of their addiction is more frightened of not having their drug of choice than they are of dying or hallucinating.

◦ ◦ ◦

When I think about a gentleman named Don, who spoke at many AA meetings, I sometimes can't believe he's the same man who was homeless on the streets for over ten years, because of his alcoholism.

I didn't know him well, and what little I did know about him was through hearing him speak about his life and struggles at AA meetings.

Most people knew and remembered him as the drunk waking up on a cold floor. Reaching for another drink was a typical routine for him. His clothes were tattered much of the time, and he wore them inside out as he staggered down the sidewalk always begging for money. Most people would walk to the other side of the street when they saw him coming.

There was usually foam dripping down his chin. His hair had not seen a comb in months or years, and no one ever saw what he looked like under his beard. His weak legs would sometimes fail him, and often he would fall flat on his face. Blood would gush down his face until it hardened on his cheeks and neck.

Many times, the local police would bring him to a shelter, where he would get cleaned up, and then he was back out in the streets to start all over again.

Alcoholism is a terrible disease. It is cunning, baffling, and insidious. Don needed to drink; that was the lie he told himself, day in and day out, and he believed it.

His body would shake until he put enough alcohol in it, often waking up by a dumpster and looking for a bite to eat in somebody's trash. He was extremely lonely and isolated. He was no longer feeling like a human being. He had no home, no real friends, no family. His best friend was booze, or so he thought.

Our thoughts are not always real and don't serve us well.

Alcohol killed him spiritually, emotionally, and mentally. He was feeling like an empty shell deep inside. I could relate to much of his story.

o o o

Alcoholics Anonymous (AA) was founded in 1935 by Bill Wilson (known as Bill W.) and Dr. Robert Smith (known as Dr. Bob). I always referred to AA as "Earth School."

Part of AA meetings in Massachusetts includes going on "commitments": going to other meetings in other towns to deliver a message of experience, strength, and hope.

One of the many commitments I did was to visit Framingham Women's Prison monthly with a friend of mine in the program who'd gotten sober in a prison.

One Wednesday a month, shoes, belts, jackets came off, and then iron gates slammed behind us, one after another. We'd sit in a room filled with women just like me: some older, some younger, some with different skin color than mine, but they were all the same as me in many aspects. Most of the women in this prison were there because of drunk driving or drugs.

I was blessed to have not been incarcerated along with them. I was blessed to have not gotten into an accident, because I too drove with alcohol in my system. I was blessed to have not gotten a DUI. I was blessed that the disease brought me to my knees at the age of twenty-two.

Some of the girls were that same age and others were grandmothers. Not all paid attention to our message, but the few who did, latched on to every word of hope that we spoke. Others in the back row were making out, talking amongst themselves, not wanting to hear the message of experience, strength, and hope we offered them.

Some of the people listening would never see outside freedom again, but they could experience *internal* freedom. I was never locked up in a prison like Framingham, but I certainly could relate to being locked up in my own prison: the prison of my distorted mind.

I was constantly reminded at each meeting I attended, just how blessed I was to know that the key to getting out of that prison was *willingness*, and I had that.

One of the many weekend retreats that I did early on in my sobriety was based on a "Course of Miracles." The only thing, the most important thing, I left with from those weekends, was a passage from the *Course of Miracles* book: "*I am not my shame. I am not my guilt, I am not my past experiences. I am a loving child of God.*"

We were also all given a wooden key that somebody had made with the word "Willingness" written on it and one of my favorite songs we sang at the end of those meetings was "Amazing Grace." It continues to be one of my favorites today.

The weekends ended with all of us getting into a big circle in the room, all holding hands, and we sang and cried through the words.

Walpole Prison was another place my group and I went to on a commitment. One time was enough for me. It was a frightening place. I may have been the only female in the room, and I do not want to know what the criminals were thinking. But I do hope something I said resonated with them, or better yet, awakened a part of them that was sleeping.

° ° °

Journal Entry:

"I am a good person. Sick, but good.

Something good and positive came over me last night. I really need to take a good look at myself and put a little of that energy that I spend on other people toward myself.

I need, and I'm starting today, to be completely honest with myself as far as my needs go. There is nothing and no one out there that can fill my real inside needs. I need to fill the inside me myself. What an awareness!

I heard that or read it a long time ago, but I didn't believe it. Or understand it. Today I do. I need your help, God, and the help of other people in the program, people who understand the mind of an alcoholic.

There are a handful of people, or one short of a handful of people, that I was getting a glimpse of, who just wanted to see me get well with no strings attached. It's time for me to start believing in myself.

I will go home and start the project of painting my apartment. I see it in my mind, but now I need to bring it to reality."

° ° °

October 6, 1991 (AA Meeting)

"Hi, my name is Connie. I have the desire to stop drinking . . . the word 'alcoholic' scares me. PJ has been a great inspiration for me since the first time I started going to AA meetings, he's shown me how to live without drinking, and that it's OK not to drink. It is possible to be accepted and liked without booze.

I am happy to be here instead of being in a pub, dreading last call, and wondering where or with whom I'd have a drink in their home, if I didn't have beer at my own home, or hoping that someone would call who would want to get high."

° ° °

Some of the meetings I attended had what was called "chip night." That was the night when various lengths of sobriety were acknowledged with a small, colored, plastic chip. The colors of the chips signified the length of sobriety in order from nine months down to six, and then to three . . . nine, six, three . . . and then one month down to twenty-four hours, or just the desire to stop drinking, with no length yet established.

At the one-year mark, and each year thereafter, a medallion was awarded. These were metal and inscribed with the number of years of sobriety for the member.

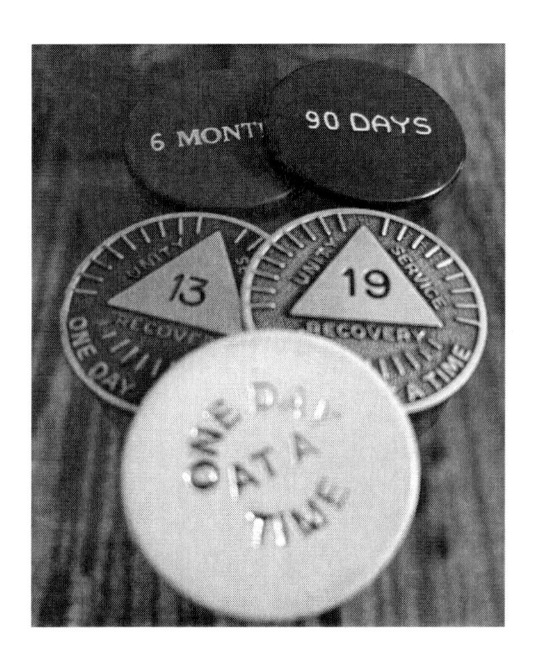

Examples of AA Medallions and Chips

I never had the courage to walk up in front of everyone to receive any chips, but my good pal PJ would mail them to me.

There was a time when one of the jobs I took in my group was to hand out the chips to people. Being a greeter at the door was the job I always avoided, as I never knew whether I'd be in the mood to talk or even shake someone's hand.

At the end of the meeting, I'd have to stand at the podium and speak into the microphone. I would always say, "Anyone want a chip and a handshake, as I'm not in a hugging mood?" It took many years, but today I enjoy giving and receiving hugs.

I felt so nervous I couldn't even think straight when an anniversary card was put in front of me. I was asked to present PJ with his three-year medallion. I was so scared, but felt so special, and I had butterflies in my tummy.

I know today that night was about him, not me, but it was a wonderful gift for me as well, since it was the first time I'd ever spoken at an AA meeting.

My Irish accent was very strong back then and I got a lot of attention afterwards for being Irish, as well as being new to recovery. I was terrified, but I also felt a different kind of high from the compliments. It felt courageous to stand up and give PJ his medallion.

° ° °

It was also suggested in AA to pray on your knees, even if you had to throw your keys under the bed as an excuse to get on your knees. This was an easy suggestion to follow since I'd grown up Catholic. The Rosary was said every night on our knees growing up, but I never developed a spiritual connection when praying.

The only connection I felt in AA was a crush on PJ. I borrowed his higher power until I developed my own.

His mother was Irish, and she was also from Galway, so I found some safety in that. We both knew that if we were to try to have anything more than a friendship, we'd screw up what we were developing, and some part of us was healthy enough to avoid that.

I remember the day I saw him walking away, holding another lady's hand. I was happy for him. I knew I would miss him. I didn't want to be with him, but I didn't want him to be with anyone else either. This was a typical thought process back then.

PJ and I met every Saturday night in my early recovery, and in the summer nights we'd go to Harvard Square. We enjoyed the street singers, especially "Flathead." He was always there with his little dog, Potato, by his side.

Ned Landin, aka "Flathead" and his dog "Potato"

PJ and I were able to continue a great friendship while his relationships with women, and mine with men, would come and go. It was so helpful to get his perspective on the male brain and to give him my version of the woman's mind.

We were nowhere near evolved enough to learn this from the people we were in relationships with. That would remain foreign for years to come.

○ ○ ○

It was March, 1991 when I got sober and I obsessed regularly, "How can I get through Christmas without drinking?" A reminder from PJ to "stay in the day" would take many years to achieve.

Being Irish, I didn't need an excuse to drink. It was in my DNA. I get more questions nowadays when I pass on having a drink, mostly, "Are you sure you're Irish?" or, "You're Irish and you don't drink?"

"No" has been my answer for over three decades now. Often that gets followed by another question, "Not even wine?"

I stand my ground, "No, not even wine."

◦ ◦ ◦

I've had many epiphanies in my life. The first was from John Bradshaw's book *Healing the Shame that Binds You.*

Prior to reading this, I was at a "shame workshop" where we were encouraged to bring in photos or cut-outs, or whatever, that would help us connect with our shame.

I felt shame throughout my life, but I could never really pinpoint it.

I brought a photo of the old, thatched house I lived in. I passed it around to the group saying, "This was my shame," but it never resonated with me. It was just words.

My first sober Christmas was uneventful in many aspects. It became just another day. I recall being invited to my boss's home for a party. It was the first time I was alone without my AA connections, at a party filled with people I knew from work and their extended families.

Downstairs was the pool room, where a dart board was set up and a bar, which I would have loved in my days of drinking. I thought it would be safer for me to mingle upstairs in the wide-open kitchen and living room with a four-sided fireplace separating the rooms. It was one of my favorite rooms in their home.

That ease was changed when I stared at a guest's glass half-filled with ice cubes, followed by a shot or two of vodka and a dash of soda. It was when she started to stir the cubes with a small straw (which is a very normal thing to do, to mix a drink) that this was no longer merely ice cubes hitting off the side of a glass. It was as loud as church bells in my ears, and I became terrified.

Vodka was one of my drugs of choice. I felt a panic like I'd never felt before. I knew I needed to get out of there. I was in my car and heading out the driveway not knowing where I was going or what I was going to do next. I didn't have a sponsor and if I did, I would not have asked them for help. I was so used to doing life alone.

I found myself driving the opposite direction from home. I was driving to PJ's house. No cell phones then, or GPS, and it was between 10 and 11 p.m. when I showed up at PJ's home, unable to talk. He just held me.

I didn't need to talk, I didn't need to explain where I was, what I was thinking or feeling. The safety I felt in his arms allowed me to sob in a way I had not done in years.

To this day, I can't pinpoint where the pain, fear, and anxiety came from. It didn't matter. What mattered was learning that my friend PJ was a safe place to fall, and I knew he wouldn't take advantage of me or ever hurt me.

God put him in my life months earlier so I would have a safe place to go.

○ ○ ○

"Your job is to stay alive, and we will do the rest." Those words, given to me by my therapist, crossed in and out of my mind at times, giving me a moment of relief. He spoke these words very early on in my journey, in *our* journey.

I found writing letters to my dad very therapeutic and an important way of establishing a relationship.

"Dear, Dear Daddy, it was a great surprise yesterday when I went to the mailbox and saw your letter. I came in and made a cuppa tea before I opened it.

'Is the kettle boiled?' is what you'd have asked.

I sat on my floor and read your letter twice. Oh, I feel so special when you write to me! I have a letter already written to you. I'll send it to you before I respond to this one.

I remember hearing I had the thrush when I was 3 or 4. I had no idea what it was at the time. Today I know it was Oral Thrush, also called oral candidiasis, and it's a condition in which the fungus Candida albicans accumulates on the lining of your mouth. It causes creamy white lesions, usually on the tongue or inner cheeks.

I have heard the story many times over the years, so I don't remember completely, but I do seem to recall some woman blowing her breath into my mouth. Supposedly, this was an old Irish cure, probably handed down from ancient druids. I still know the house where she lived, and I can only assume her gift worked since the thrush went away.

I also remember taking Noreen's son when he was two and a half or 3 to another lady who was said to use the same cure. Noreen and I took him 3 days in a row, and she blew into his mouth, down his throat.

We were in and out of her home in under ten minutes. I didn't remember if there was an exchange of money or not. We both just saw how much pain her little guy was in. He loved his bottle, but his mouth was so sore from ulcers that he was not able to tolerate even the rubber teat from his dummy, his favorite thing in the world. By day three he was cured, and it was never to return.

I remember how safe and comfortable sleeping between you and Mammy felt. It was the safest place in the world. You and Mammy would not hurt me in bed and I truly believe neither of you ever hurt me intentionally. You can't teach what you didn't know.

There are times even now when I close my eyes and try to imagine that I am between you and Mammy, to relive that feeling of safety and comfort.

I'm coming up on my 19-month sobriety date. I haven't had a drop of alcohol in 19 months. I feel so much better I can't describe the good feelings sometimes.

I love the way you were able to express your feelings with me in your letter. Have you ever shared your feelings with anybody before? I felt bad when you shared how you were out by the gate of the old house, waiting for me to come home. I didn't think I even knew you were worried. You never showed your feelings, never said anything to me. You would hide them back then. You would hide when you heard someone coming, so I didn't know you were worried about me. I'm truly sorry for any worries or uneasy feelings I brought to you and Mammy. I was selfish at the time and had no idea how my actions impacted you. I was unable to feel your care back then.

I am getting into playing golf now. I will send you a picture soon. We have not seen each other in five years.

Anytime I think of that, my eyes fill up with water. I love you, Daddy, more than anything in this world.

I am at work right now, so I'm going to write about something else. I can't have tears in my eyes at work.

It's only been in the past year and a half that I've been looking at myself and trying to get to know who I am. I felt empty as a child.

My eyes are still admired a couple of times a week, and I always mention to people that I have your eyes. People tell me I have a nice smile. People are nice to me and I'm nice to people too and I know I didn't learn that in the pubs. These were qualities I picked up from you and Mammy, not the barroom.

Do you remember the Christmas we were still in the old house? Santa Claus had come and gone, and we got Legos that Christmas. I was getting a piggyback ride or shoulder ride from Patsy and he slipped on the Lego, he fell and landed on my ankle and I broke it. Willie Small, the Lord have Mercy on him R.I.P, brought me to Acton . . . he was driving a black Morris Minor at the time.

I was not sure if Acton was his first name or last but there was no 'Dr' in front of it, he was also a bonesetter for animals. I believe most other people would have been taken to the ER for an X-ray and a cast. Mammy put a scarf around my head, and I sat on her lap in the front seat. It was a comfortable ride despite my head was touching the roof of the car.

You asked me if I remember Martin Scully. I remember his name. I don't remember his face. I remember being at his funeral and each of the daughters dropped a red rose down on the coffin, one-by-one. Hard to believe it was thirteen years ago. I was ten years old at the time and we were still living in the old house, with the small windows. The stained lace curtains got washed for 'The Stations' (Mass at the house).

I remember washing the cement floors sometimes at three in the morning with Johnny. I loved doing that and especially with him. I felt a great connection with him when we were young, not through words as we didn't talk much, but he let me into his world from time to time. He was an amazing artist, and he would show only me his work. I felt special. We are older now, so we are getting to know each other again. I wish we were young again sometimes so I would still feel that closeness, but that's not possible. The memories will always be with me, the bad memories, and the good ones. I love reading the stories you shared about me when I was younger, please keep sharing them.

I am hoping to get my green card this time around. Maybe I'll be lucky, please God. I have applied the last two years when they were offering them but was not contacted. Not my time.

If I am meant to have one, I believe I will get it. I really believe we're all put on this earth for a reason and I'm trying just to live for today. I have no idea what my purpose is today, but I know it was not to be a drunk on the streets of Boston.

I don't get to go to Mass every Sunday because of work, but I do believe in God and believe he was and always will be with me. Mass is an hour long here, 30 minutes there. I like that better. God must be in a hurry at home or he knows we are quick learners. Or maybe he knows we can only retain a little. If we could only know what He's thinking.

The weather is getting cold now. The trees are so beautiful. I will send you some pictures of them soon. Are you looking forward to Christmas?"

I don't want to put up the Christmas tree this year. They are selling decorations for Christmas already. There is another big holiday coming up here soon called Thanksgiving. It's the last Thursday in November.

Everyone gets together and has a big turkey and endless amounts of food. We never celebrated that day at home, so it really does not mean a lot to me.

I'll be working that day anyway. I like being invited to people's homes, but I never go. I feel like a hermit who likes people at times.

It's getting busy at work now. I'll write some more soon.

Your Dearest Daughter,

Connie"

As I read back over my writings from the early sober years, I'm reminded of just how scared I was of everything. Many times, I wrote about my fear of someone being nice to me at a meeting, especially a male. I always wondered what he wanted.

I was also aware I knew I had stopped growing mentally and emotionally years earlier when the abuse started. Most of my writings in '92 involved wishing I were more mature.

AA meetings were a very big part of my life back then, as I knew it was where the medicine was for my alcoholic mind.

An AA meeting was always on my plate, two meetings some days, to clear my mind or to try to feel more human. Many times, I'd leave a meeting early, as my anxiety was too high. If my friend Theresa was there, or PJ, it was easier to stay the entire hour.

Many times, when I was at the Saturday night meeting, at St. Elizabeth's Hospital in Brighton, MA, it was an hour long and there was always a break for the collection, or to get coffee, tea, and of course sugar in the form of cookies.

I sometimes walked to the little church by myself, on nights with no meetings, not because I was a good Catholic, but because it was small, dark, and rarely had anyone there at 8.30 p.m. I felt safe in the dark and alone. It felt like a comfortable, familiar place.

I always went to meetings late and left early to avoid interacting with people. So, one night, instead of returning to the meeting, I went to visit Martina. She's still a good friend today. She eventually made her home in Galway with her husband and three kids. But that night, she was still single and living in Boston, about half an hour's drive away.

She was not at home, so I went to the Village Pub and there she was. I think that was where I wanted to be as well. It was a feeling of home. I stayed with her and we went to another bar and had dinner, but no drinks.

Bulimia had been awakened a few months before, so when I came home, I threw up and felt better. It took a long time to fall asleep, but I was sober.

○ ○ ○

September 12, 1992

"Today was an ok day, Thank God, a refreshing change.

I felt like sharing at the meeting tonight, so I did. I was nervous but ok, and I said what was supposed to come out, even if I had something different in mind at the beginning.

My thoughts are changing at 100 MPH. I feel I have accepted that I was sexually abused as a child and that my inner child needs to grow. I need constant reassurance that 'you are a good person.' Today, this moment, I do believe and feel that I am."

September 13, 1992

"Today I feel so lonely, so not sexy, and fat. Please help me, God."

September 14, 1992

"Still tired, but I need to get the house cleaned up and I'm glad I didn't resort to overeating and purging tonight, like I did last night. Please God keep me going, thank you."

September 15, 1992

"Pretty good day at work. Worked until 4pm. Went to visit a neighbor of mine, Eileen. She's here from Galway

visiting her son and his family. She looks great, she is a sweetheart.

Eileen shared sad news about Annette Ford. Annette had drowned, and her body was not yet found. Please God, help the family. Annette and I were close in National School.

Went to a meeting and then to UNO's where I purged my food after. Feeling so ashamed to find a man sexually attractive, but it also has a good feeling attached to it. At times, it can feel as powerful as the desire to use, or drink. I feel numb."

September 20, 1992

"Tomorrow, I will be in America five years. Since I got sober, I am more aware of being illegal, but it is what it is."

September 25, 1992

I need to call home soon, I haven't in a few weeks.

Not a good day overall. I felt fat and ugly all day, no matter what I wear, how tanned I am, or that my top clothing is 'Medium' and my pants are a size 8. I didn't throw up, so I guess that's good.

Denise, a friend from AA, is so sick from her anorexia. Her legs are bruised, she is weak and losing her voice. She needs 'round-the-clock help. I gave her my number, but I may never hear from her. It feels good to not always be thinking about myself. It is in giving that we receive."

° ° °

It's important to remember that the mind of an alcoholic is in a constant state of flip-flopping. It's like feeling grateful to be sober in the morning, and later that same day, craving the drink. Trains of thought are convoluted, bouncing around, and often get derailed. That is the insidious nature of the disease and it shows up in my journal entries like breadcrumbs left to follow back in time to when my thoughts were rattled.

° ° °

Thursday, October 1, 1992

"Please God help me find extra work or money. Will go to a meeting later. I hate when I put others before myself. I have never felt as emotional in all my life. I thought I had lost my life and a new job and the trip to the Bahamas were off the table. But, I didn't. I am going there for 2 weeks.

What I've learned is that I need to remember the most important person in my life is me. I need to put my energy in me and not in other people. I have to be selfish, but not hurt others along the way."

November 14, 1992

"Today is one of the happiest days I ever dreamt of. Daddy came to visit me in America. I have not seen him in five years. WOW! So, keep in mind that my dad would rarely even look up at an airplane, never mind get in one and come to America. Clearly his love is more powerful than his fear, even if the 'L' word is not used often.

I knew Mammy was coming. This would have been her third trip in the five years since I left home. It was the best surprise ever!

Feeling lost lately, but that's ok. I don't have to drink!

My personality has changed so much lately. What used to be fun is no longer my truth. Drinking rarely let me into real fun. It may have started out that way years earlier, or maybe the first hour or two in the evening, but fun is never how I would describe how I felt at 2am.

I actually have some peace of mind, I'm sure this too shall pass."

o o o

My personality had changed and my thinking had changed, about everything.

What used to be good and fun was no longer my truth. One of the lowest times in my drug use, and the kinds of people that were in my life, entered my mind from time to time.

The one that rings the loudest was being at my apartment with a female friend, another user, not really a friend, as we were not capable of a true friendship. She was big into cocaine, which I dabbled in for a year, but it was expensive, and I had fears that it would take me elsewhere.

She called her connection who sold us weed. It was my birthday, and he came with a bag of it. The payment was her giving him a blowjob. I felt like I was in a movie. I had never stooped that low myself, but this was how she paid for the weed.

After a few minutes he was satisfied. He left and she handed me the bag and said, "Happy Birthday." I was numb. Dissociation was a familiar place for me to be. We rolled a couple of joints and proceeded to get high.

A week or two later a knock came to my door. Same guy. Luckily, I kept my foot behind the door as I opened it a few inches. He looked strung out. I felt scared. I don't know what he wanted, but I asked him to leave.

He attempted to push the door open, but my foot blocked it and I locked it shut seconds later. He continued to knock on the door in anger.

I was friends with someone who was in the "business" of dealing with people like him. He was spoken to once within twenty-four hours and I never saw him again.

° ° °

I had no relationships back in Ireland. Men were attracted to me. Some were married who made passes at me and more. My wiring was so crossed that if a guy made a pass at me and didn't take it further, I would automatically wonder, *What's wrong with me, why didn't he like me?*

More than likely, they had a moment of clarity and thought I was young enough to be their daughter. With those that did take it further, I wouldn't enjoy the physical aspect of it, but loved the attention that came with it. I loved feeling desired and that translated to love for me.

I was twenty, almost twenty-one (chronologically) when I was involved with a forty-nine-year-old man. He was not abusive. Maybe lonely or bored in his own life, but not abusive. I had no idea how to be a girlfriend, or a friend for that matter. I was still drinking at the time with very disruptive thoughts and crossed wiring.

It ended when I got sober.

One of the first real feelings that came alive was that I didn't want human touch. My body had no idea how it would react. Many times, it didn't know the difference between good and bad touch.

I was not able to be honest with myself and therefore with him. We would make plans and I just wouldn't show up. He eventually got the idea that it was over.

Even holding hands at the end of an AA meeting for the Lord's Prayer, or a Serenity Prayer, was a trigger for me. It was a touch I couldn't handle.

Back then, I couldn't imagine ever having a normal, healthy relationship. Even if I had read what that looks like, I don't think I would have understood it. I was in constant judgment of my body.

My life would never have turned out the way it has if I did not put the booze and drugs down. It was the greatest gift I got from whom I call God today! A gift of desperation, some would call it.

Growing up Catholic and praying to God every day, one would think my connection was solid. When I got in that plane to America with my two best friends, Martina and Booze, I left God. I don't think I ever really had Him.

He had me, though, and never abandoned me.

One of the many one-liners I heard in AA was, "If you're having a hard time with God, imagine the hard time he's having with you." It always made me laugh.

I had zero connection to anything. Booze was my only "go-to" in the end. I had drinking buddies, a few acquaintances, and a handful of friends, but none of them knew much about me.

I didn't know much about myself, either. Staying clean and sober will always be my backbone.

ABUSE

Abuse has many faces. It can be quiet and sinister or loud and violent. It also becomes a secret, and secrets live in the dark.

I read in one of the many self-help books I purchased since I got sober:

Your childhood is stolen once you've been abused.

I do not and did not deserve it. I just had to endure it.

Was this what feeling cared for really was? Was this what "feeling liked" was supposed to feel like? The fear was overwhelming. The thoughts racing through my head felt like they were going to create an explosion. A child should not have to live like that.

Just walking towards my uncle's house on a Saturday morning, I would turn around the corner to the house and see his car. The fear was immediate. It was like someone poured concrete into me. I was frozen.

When his car was not there, I'd feel safe until noon, an hour of freedom, until the afternoon. This fear would come home with me and it would take over my entire body.

° ° °

"What am I supposed to feel, God? What is that feeling? Please help me, God.

Please, God, help me grow while I sleep.

Fear can keep a child frozen and numb from the pain, like shivering in a cold rain, cleansing her skin, but not feeling clean.

Do this with me, God. I need to do some deep work that is extremely scary and painful. Please do it with me.

This year, I'm going to look back at my collage book of my old memories, feelings, and thoughts to help me get in touch with the fear of the abuse, the hidden fear.

Do this with me, God.

It's time to feel the fear, the terror behind the darkness and silence. Please, God, help me deal with the part of me that liked it, that liked the attention behind the touch. Help me through this fear."

° ° °

My lips were sealed for twenty-two years.

I was frozen inside. Dead, dark inside.

Once the touching ends, the physical part is over, but the mental, spiritual, and emotional damage lasts a lifetime. Being sexually violated on a regular basis does more to the mind than the body.

I was nineteen the last time I was violated/raped. It was an Irish man who was engaged to be married a few months later. I had a few drinks in me but wasn't drunk. I regressed to being a helpless child, as I begged him with a quiet voice, "Stop, please stop. Please stop!" He didn't listen, and it didn't last long.

I drank for the next three days straight to bury it with all the other memories.

He was a roommate of a good friend. We never talked about it, but I believe she knew. It was not until my therapist referred to this as "rape" four years later that I began to use that word to describe it. Today I still use the same definition.

The abuse did have an uncomfortable physical component to it. It didn't leave bruises, but memories, body memories, and the deep scars that it leaves in the mind last a lifetime. The triggers years later, when I was eventually able to date a man, and learn what trust and love were, continued to haunt me and affect my sexual life with my partner for many years.

"It truly is the longest journey from our head to our hearts" -Sioux Indian saying.

I was sharing the experience of abuse by my uncle with a cousin here in the U.S. and she helped me determine how old I was, or may have been, when the abuse started. She had memories of my uncle being inappropriate with her, as well, when she was in Ireland at the age of three.

When I try to remember an age, the thought that comes to mind is, "I don't remember him any other way."

He would always find a way to get me alone. Some of the times his own children were in the room also. His fingers would always find their way inside my pants, my jeans. He would say loudly as he would grab my breast, "I know Connie doesn't like this." I became his prey.

Rarely, he'd leave me alone and so in those rare moments I'd escape his hand and fingers inside me and my pants.

My uncle lived with my grandmother, and my mom went to visit them a couple of times a month. My sister and I would often go with her and we vacationed there in the summers, my brothers more so than me. We would take two busses and walk three miles to get to their home, but my uncle would always drive us home at night.

I often was the one to sit in the front seat between him and the passenger as it was not an actual seat, more like a bench. The gear shift was between my legs, another chance for him to feel me outside my underwear if I was wearing a skirt, or through my pants.

One cousin's nickname for him was "crotch grabber." Having my crotch grabbed became such a normal price to pay during my visits. You could almost guarantee my crotch would be touched as I walked by him many times, and he always had a grin on his face.

I loved it when his car was not in the driveway, when we walked around the corner to his house. "Safe for a few hours" was what my body was feeling.

He often worked half a day on a Saturday, but he would always come home. And I would always get abused. My mom was never in the room or she would be engaged somewhere with her own mom.

The adults—his wife, my mom, and my grandmother—called it "messing." "He's just messing around." He messed around with me for years, from maybe four years old on. I learned at a very young age what my value was: it was in my vagina and boobs.

His wife, too, would often recite the same statement, "Stop messing with the kids," but he had so much joy and laughter on his face, no one could make him stop.

I also witnessed physical abuse from the hands of his wife. I stood paralyzed, as I watched the heads of her sons being slammed repeatedly against a concrete wall. Their crime was that they were looking for food too late at night, aggravating her to the point of madness. But that is not my story to tell.

Grabbing my crotch was as normal as a high-five on the streets in America. It would start outside the clothing, jeans or skirt, and his hand would always make its way inside. His finger would slide back and forth on my vagina, and always inside me.

He knew I didn't like it, but I can still see the grin on his face as he was getting pleasure from it. He always smiled. No words. He would pull his hand out if someone came into the room. It was often in the kitchen where the TV, stove, and big table with the ketchup and mustard sat in a brown Tupperware container. I still despise both smells from them today and have never tasted either one.

He would be outside the bathroom when I would finish, waiting to grab me again. Sometimes, I would hurry back to where my mom was, so I would not be alone with him. It was never forced, but I also felt I never had a choice. I had to take it. I was silent. I never complained or told anyone. I didn't know it was wrong, but it didn't feel right either. There was no one who could help me.

My dad was never with us during those visits. I might have sat next to him if he was there and felt safe. My mom was often visiting the neighbors as this was the village she grew up in.

I had my dad on a pedestal for many years, as he was the one man in the family that I knew would never touch me inappropriately. This should be the norm for all children. My brothers and most of the neighbors were also good souls and not abusers.

◦ ◦ ◦

Dr. Nolan rarely smiled and to a child, he was scary looking.

Square glasses sat on his nose with thin silver frames. He had a habit of saying, "Oh yeah . . ." He was an intimidating, tall man that I never felt comfortable or safe with, but I didn't know that was how I felt at the time.

Most of my visits to him meant enduring him pushing his—what I know today as his erect penis—against me. Before he let me out of his office, back to the waiting area where my mom would be, he would have one hand against the door and his other hand on my lower back and the top of my buttocks.

His hands were huge. One covered most of my lower back. His hand pushed my body into his hard penis. At the time it just felt like a hard thing as I had no idea what it was.

Dr. Nolan was always in a suit, most of them dark grey in color, matching his short, dark hair, with grey on the sides. He was over six feet tall and seemed like seven feet when I was a child. One leg was always bent back when he sat on his chair writing a prescription when I needed one.

Unfortunately, I had to frequently visit Dr. Nolan due to my asthma and each time, I would endure being violated. And like most victims of sexual abuse, I learned to keep that secret, too.

Dr. Nolan's office was part of his home and his visiting hours for patients were from 10 a.m. to 2 p.m. and 6 to 8 p.m., no appointment necessary, first come, first served.

My dad had him on a pedestal, because one Christmas Day, Dr. Nolan treated my dad's asthma in his home dispensary. As a result of that, my dad went to his grave never knowing how the doctor had violated his daughter. I kept it secret from my mom as well.

I didn't want to hurt my parents or their image of the doctor. Other abusers were neighbors and a man I babysat for.

Dr. Nolan is dead.

° ° °

Here is a letter I wrote, but never sent to my parents . . .

"Dear Mammy and Daddy,

How's it going? It was good to talk to you last week, Mammy, it was a good feeling to be able to talk to you longer than two minutes about my ongoing struggle of the effects of being sexually abused. I bought the Sunday World and was able to read what you were talking about. The painful stories of the people who were abused when they were little people. Young innocent little people. The reason why they did not say anything then was they were scared and felt nobody would believe them. They were also too young to know what was happening to them. They did not have any words or a voice to say what was going on.

Now that they are adults, they are able to talk. This also describes what I was feeling. I remember the first time I tried talking with you about what my uncle, your brother, had done to me. You were not able to believe me and I know how painful it was. You didn't want to hear it and you told me it was all in my mind.

I also remembered your question, 'Why would you say that about him, he wouldn't do that.' I do know how hard it was for you both to accept it.

I have carried that secret with me for so long. When I used to drink or do drugs, I would be able to forget the pain. When I stopped drinking, the pain was there waiting for me. I have been feeling a lot of pain the past four years. The confusing thoughts, the understanding I have of love, etc. I wish you could have believed ME, but it took a priest's story to have you understand what I was saying. You were able to take the word of a priest but not your own daughter.

I have cut out some stuff from the paper that I could have written in my own story. Please take the time to read it. There is one sentence here that describes what Dr. Nolan used to do to me. He would not let me leave the room without making me put my hands around his neck and would rub himself against me.

Yes, Dr. Nolan. That was why I hated him so much. I hated going to see him. He used to block the entrance with his hand until he got some of those hugs. He may also say I am making it up. Why would someone make something like that up?

The important thing right now is that I am not carrying these secrets with me. It was not my fault. They were the adults, not me. It was not my fault. For years I blamed myself for the abuse. I felt the shame. I carried the guilt. There were times I felt so bad about what happened I wanted to die. There were times before I stopped drinking that I would ask God to let me die in my sleep. I am grateful today that he didn't hear me. I have learned to talk to a counselor.

It is like it says in the paper. In counseling, you go back to the time when the little girl you once were, was being abused. I can't put into words how painful that is. That is also how to heal. I am working towards the freedom that real people have who have never been abused. I will never have that freedom completely. The damage that occurs is unbelievable. I can relate to the pain that is shared in both situations, in both cases in the paper. The action was a little different, but the feelings are the same.

It was great to read in an Irish newspaper something that has been going on for years, to come out. NO MORE SECRETS. NO MORE PROTECTING THE PRIESTS AND OTHER ABUSERS. IT HAS TO STOP. IT HAS TO STOP NOW. WE CAN NOT LET ANY OTHER INNOCENT LITTLE PEOPLE BE ABUSED LIKE I WAS. NOREEN HAS ALSO SUFFERED FROM THIS. NO MORE SECRETS. I HOPE THE PAIN THAT I HAVE SUFFERED WILL SOMEDAY HELP OTHER LITTLE PEOPLE TO SPEAK UP. I AM AN ADULT TODAY. MY UNCLE WILL NEVER HURT ME AGAIN AND IF WHAT I HAVE DONE—'TALK ABOUT IT'—WILL PREVENT SOMEONE ELSE FROM GETTING HURT, THEN IT WAS WORTH IT.

There was a time when I thought that you would never believe me. Even the loneliness was worth it.

What this letter is all about is, in a way, to thank you for your understanding.

One other thing that is so important to do when something is not right, is to talk about it. Even with each other, you need to communicate. I know it was not something we ever did growing up. If you looked alright on the outside, then you were ok. That's not true. So much can happen behind your back or behind closed doors.

There are times when I wish you could have made him stop. I was too scared to say anything. Sometimes I get angry. I can't do anything about the past. I can't change it, but I am working towards recovering from it."

DR. MARK FANGER, ED.D., CST, CGP

I didn't know if I would make the cut.

I didn't know if he wanted to work with me. I didn't know if I was good enough or if I had enough issues for him to deal with.

Today I know my therapist, Dr. Fanger, took three weeks to decide to work with me. I was, in my mind and body, broken beyond repair, my wiring was crossed, with one year of sobriety under my belt.

I later learned the three weeks of questioning was so that he could assess whether he was skilled enough to deal with my trauma issues.

One of the few questions I asked him in this early stage was, "Do you think I need therapy?" And he answered, "You could fill a room with therapists with what you have shared with me." Most people might have been offended by that answer, but I felt relief. I felt I was home.

I grew up chronologically in Ireland, but I really grew up in my therapist's office in Newton, Massachusetts.

Rigorous honesty was the technique that allowed me to overcome everything I had encountered.

It meant telling the truth when it's easier to lie and sharing thoughts and feelings even when there may be consequences.

In twelve-step recovery at AA, the requirement is to take a fearless and personal inventory and promptly admit to any dishonesty.

My favorite definition of rigorous honesty was one I'd heard at an AA meeting in Galway, Ireland. The man's name was Gabriel. He sat on the left-hand side of the room smoking his pipe. His message came back to Boston with me, and I've shared it ever since when occasion arises.

He said, "The difference between honesty and rigorous honesty: Honesty is when you tell the neighbor you stole a rope and rigorous honesty is you tell him there was a cow attached to the end of the rope."

I made a commitment to myself when I started therapy with Dr. Mark Fanger that I was going to be honest. It was the first time in my life that I said those words.

It took time to become rigorously honest. I had to learn how to tell the entire truth. I would not think I was lying but leaving out a big part of the story was in fact not being fully truthful.

This was one of the many, many life lessons Mark taught me over the years.

∘ ∘ ∘

One of the homework tasks Mark gave me, in the first year of our journey together, was to rent and watch the movie *My Left Foot*. I remember seeing it like it was yesterday. It was about a boy named Christy Brown who was born into a working-class Irish family.

He was a spastic quadriplegic, basically paralyzed, and at age five he could control his left foot to the point where he could use chalk between his toes to scrawl words on the floor. With the help of his mother, Christy overcame his condition and became a painter, poet, and actor.

I believe Dr. Fanger was trying to teach me what an emotionally, spiritually, and physically "plugged-in" mother looked like.

I laughed at how ridiculous it was to have me watch such a fake movie. I was trying to educate Dr. Fanger about *real* Irish mammys. I told him mothers like Christy's did not exist. These were mere actors.

He knew that I may have understood the definition of the word "affection" and the meaning of "being there" emotionally for a loved one, but he also knew I had zero idea what it looked or felt like growing up. My home environment was filled with emotional constipation.

That movie did display a very powerful, relentless love for a child, and that notion was not even in my wildest dreams. Today, it all makes sense that what Dr. Fanger was teaching me was what he knew I lacked. I think I was also teaching him.

My therapy appointments were every Wednesday at 11 a.m. and every check I wrote was to "Dr. Fanger." It was a year and a half into the therapy when one Wednesday morning, as I sat in the waiting area, a colleague of his walked out of his office and said, "See you later, Mark."

Fear awakened inside me like I'd never felt before. Hearing someone call him by his first name instead of "doctor" changed him somehow in my mind into a man.

Dr. Fanger was no longer asexual. For the year and a half before that moment, the necessary trust between us developed because I never viewed him as a man. He was just Dr. Fanger. I spent most of our session that day asking him the same questions repeatedly, "Your name is Mark? You're a man? You're a guy?"

Clearly, it wasn't news to him that he was a man, but it took our therapy to a deeper place.

Attracting sick souls had become my way of life. Attracting men who validated my distorted beliefs in myself, and quietly doubting the ones who didn't see me in that light.

Soon familiar questions came to my mind as I sat across from Mark: "What's wrong with me?" "Why doesn't he like me that way [like my uncle did]?" "Am I not good enough?"

I was so damaged.

When these thoughts emerged with Mark in therapy, I had the courage to ask him those same questions. Mark, Dr. Fanger, reassured me he would never see me in that light even if I wanted him to. I was happy and sad. Excited and scared. My wonder was, how will he ever really get to know me if he doesn't touch me?

I continued with these questions surfacing many, many times in my early healing days. I didn't understand that he didn't need to touch me physically to know me, and I also didn't understand that to touch me, didn't mean he would know me.

These distorted thoughts were eventually turned around as I continued to heal my brokenness.

I don't know if I would have predicted it that day, but I spent fifty minutes EVERY week with Mark Fanger for seventeen years, except when he would take that long, seemingly endless month-long vacation in the fall, usually to Cape Cod. I thought about the movie with Robert De Niro and Billy Crystal, *Analyze This*, and how De Niro's character followed his therapist on vacation, but I didn't think Mark would appreciate me showing up.

My healthier side was baffled, but I realized that over the years, the time I had with Mark, weekly without fail, and every Wednesday at 11 a.m. . . . that was MY time.

I was learning to trust for the first time in my life.

I didn't know what trust was or what it felt like until then. I was so fragmented. I lived with two very different thoughts about the same experience: I felt broken beyond repair, yet somehow felt I could be broken and still feel OK in his company, in his office.

When I started my journey with Mark, he saw beyond my thoughts and feelings. Most of my writings back then were to God and about my therapy.

Today I understand I was coming alive for maybe the first time in my life. My feelings and thoughts were thawing out.

An example of my feelings returning to their rightful place, one that I vividly remember, was driving to the gym one morning. I was at a red light behind a school bus filled with what looked like six-, seven-, eight-year-olds heading off somewhere fun for the day.

A couple of the little boys gave me the peace sign, and when I responded with a big smile and two peace signs back, their energy heightened. I was behind them for a mile or two. It reminded me of the time I was in the back of a bus at that age and being excited when a driver behind us would acknowledge me.

I overtook them on the highway to see their little arms waving out the window. It made my day much brighter and by the looks on their little faces, I may have done the same for them. I had no idea how much attention I was starving for when I was their age. I wanted to be seen as a person, not as a body, but my uncle and other men like him only saw my body, the only thing that was ever acknowledged.

I was starved for recognition from male strangers to validate my existence. The waves from strange men in cars sometimes filled that void in those moments. I would say to Dr. Fanger that I was "empty." He would remind me that the emptiness is filled with pain and sadness.

"Empty" felt easier for me to feel, but eventually he walked metaphorically with me into each room in my mind to address the pain, loneliness, and sadness I had buried deep inside.

He told me one day, "Your job is to stay alive, and we will do the rest." I remember hearing the word "we" and liking how it sounded, and he was a man of his word.

December 7, 1995

> *"Tonight is my last night of being twenty-six years old.*
>
> *When I wake up tomorrow, I will be twenty-seven years old. It will be a new beginning for the New Year. God is going to continue caring. I need you always to walk with me. Please continue with your guidance.*
>
> *I will continue asking. I'm learning about God, curious about Him and faith. What control I have and what I don't.*
>
> *I've learned a lot in a very short time, and I look forward to more data. The data I've gathered thus far is not serving me well. It's a process of unlearning and learning.*
>
> *Thank you, God, for putting people in place to guide me where I need to go."*

o o o

One of the tools I developed in my early recovery was writing to myself. Part of that process was to integrate with a fragment of myself that I'd disowned for years. I called her (the fragment), my inner child, "Little Connie."

One of our goals was to become integrated with many parts of me that were fragmented. The diagnosis of Post-Traumatic Stress Disorder (PTSD) made this clear, but quite complicated at times.

"Little Connie" and my adult self, needed to integrate. I knew it would not be pleasant or fun, but it was essential. Many of the sessions moving forward involved me sitting on the floor without my shoes, so I could feel more in touch with my younger self.

Another Wednesday with Mark, and fifteen minutes of the way through, there was excitement in his eyes. They were so alive, and it was so real for me. He started my session by talking about fear and asking how "Little Connie" felt when she was yelled at, the kid demanding my attention, and I stared back at him, "She feels scared and wants to run."

"To: Connie

From: Little Connie

February 7, 1995

I am sad and lonely inside . . . we thought we'd go to the gym every day . . . you put make-up on my face . . . you keep trying to change the outsides, but I'm still hurting inside. So lonely . . . I feel so alone it hurts. Mark wants to get you to know me so please, Connie, help me to come out. I really want to get better, but I am afraid of getting hurt again and I am afraid of Mark because he is a man.

Mark wants to help me, not hurt me. I want his help so bad but I'm so scared.

The lonely feelings hurt, but the fear is a stronger hurt . . . please let me out . . . I feel I like am in the dark . . . it's so dark where I am . . . it's where I live alone even when the lights are on. You don't let me play, sing, dance, or run around . . . you don't let me be a kid. Why don't you let me free? I want freedom. I need freedom . . . other kids have it and they even want me to join them . . . then you won't let me.

Why don't you let me? Why am I living in this dark hole? Don't just give me food . . . too much food and then make me get rid of it. I want to feel loved. I want to feel . . . I want to feel. I need your help. Will you help me please? Let Mark help you and me. I'm comfortable with the way he dresses every week . . . he's always at the office waiting for me and I like the way he wears his pants, shirt, socks, and sandals . . . I don't know about the way he came upstairs last week with jacket, shades, and glasses . . . he smiled, but he was not the same . . . he was a big man but with a warm smile . . . I'm glad he smiles if you did not :-)

I think I would be afraid of him. I don't know why I'm afraid of Mark, because I know he will never hurt me . . . but he's still a man. What do you think this man is going to do? I don't know. When I think of Mark, I think of the one I trust and care about, but then I think about the man being that same guy. It feels different.

I want to believe that Mark is not going to hurt me."

When I first started therapy, I was totally convinced that I was nothing more than boobs and a vagina, as that was all that had ever received validation throughout my life as a child and teenager.

I was so much more than that.

Dr. Fanger became my parent, mentor, teacher, advisor, and I know he loved me in a way I was never loved to that point before. It was a healthy, professional, real, genuine, respectful love.

The healing took place in his office. It was a safe space, a space without judgment, a space where I was encouraged and supported to share my truth.

Perception is truth.

I now know five people can grow up in the same house, with the same parents, and have five entirely different perceptions of what went on under the same roof and come away with totally different ideas about themselves.

Dr. Fanger cared for me before I could care for myself. I continue being grateful to him and I call him each year on my sobriety anniversary: March 14, 1991, the start of me living a sober life. I call him to make sure he doesn't forget me and to say thank you.

We usually have a playful joke to share with one another. Every year I call him, leaving him a voicemail, reminding him who I am, including my full name, knowing full well he'd recognize my voice anyway. His message back to me is always something like, "This was your therapist, Dr. Mark Fanger, in case YOU forgot." It always brings a smile to my face.

Sometimes I would be driving on Route 128, heading home, when something I'd recall he said would register. One of the many lessons he taught me was how to be "comfortable enough being uncomfortable."

He also made it clear that the work I had to do around the abuse might have been easier to do with a female therapist, and he gave me that option. He knew that just the fact he was a male, would make the work more difficult. He was right. I declined the female alternative. I wanted to work only with him. I also had zero experience with a female as my mom was emotionally absent. Despite the male connections I had with men that were abusive, it was still a connection, nonetheless.

I had also learned how to trust him before we did the deeper work, when I shared the sick secrets that were making me toxic.

We are only as sick as our secrets. Trust is imperative to do this work.

The shame and guilt of the secrets that I carried deeply, didn't belong to me. They belonged to the abusers, who should have been carrying them instead, not me.

I also said to him our first session, *"Do not tell me I need medication,"* as a previous therapist that I had seen for five weeks put me on Prozac after one session. He wanted to give me more medication and after six weeks I didn't go back. Maybe I did need it. But after that session, I knew at some level he was not the right doctor for me.

I stayed on the Prozac that was prescribed by him for a few months. I was afraid to get off of it, but I had a fear of being on it, as well. The reality is, I was newly sober and like most newly sober people, I was also depressed. I felt like I was going crazy.

Dr. Fanger respected my wishes, but he did mention a few times over the next several years, that my journey may have been easier or less dark had I decided to take antidepressants. I was stubborn and wanted to do it without drugs. I didn't like and don't like side effects, and most medication does carry side effects.

He also reminded me that my stubbornness saved my life, but then the time came when that same power—for the lack of a better word—was getting in the way of my recovery. I needed to learn to be vulnerable. I hated being vulnerable. I hated needing him.

A major part of my journey was to go through that process of learning how to depend on someone and have that someone be there for me. For a period of time, he let me call and check in with him every day and it would last twenty to thirty seconds, if that. He was teaching me what it felt like to have somebody there, a lesson I've carried with me throughout my journey. I'm not sure how long or how many months he allowed this, but it was exactly what I needed at that time.

He knew the depth of my abandonment issues, even though my parents were always home. My dad worked on the farm and my mom was a housewife. I shared a bed with them for the first twelve years of my life, yet I felt alone and never learned to reach out for help.

My parents' toolboxes were extremely limited when it came to knowing how to be present for me, but I still wouldn't trade them for any other parents in the world today.

o o o

During my drinking days, it meant nothing to me to walk away from people, anyone, even when they were passed out and could have used help. It felt natural, like a normal behavior. Any relationships I had were meaningless. And this behavior was carried into my early recovery.

I was a year sober before I learned to say goodbye at the end of my shift to my co-workers. It was only after I was asked to do so by my boss, who thought I was upset with my colleagues. I was baffled and didn't see what the big deal was in just leaving without saying goodnight. I get it today: "hello" and "goodbye" are normal gestures when one enters and leaves a home, or job.

That's how screwed-up my thinking was back then.

That same boss was a wonderful soul and gave me a job when I was un-documented. We became friends and she too cared for me long before I could care for myself.

She had a loving heart, and she knew how to feel it and express it. I questioned her love for me as I had no foundation, understanding, or appreciation for it. "Why does she like me?" For a long time, I didn't hear an answer from the same mind that created the question.

That changed about a year and a half or two years into therapy. I was at my gym sitting at the juice bar when I was hit by an amazing emotion. I felt warmth for the first time in my heart and that was my first glimpse of how it felt to feel care or love for another human being.

In that moment I felt my heart begin to thaw out from years of frozen feelings. I remember making a call to my friend, my boss, and saying to her, "I know why you love me." She had no idea what I was saying or where I was coming from and even after I explained it, it was way over her head.

In time, I shared different parts of my childhood with her and one of the most supportive statements she ever said to me was, "I have no idea what your life felt like growing up."

I knew she couldn't comprehend that kind of a life. She grew up in a supportive atmosphere, but it was refreshing to know her truth. She didn't need to understand it or understand how I was feeling. She just loved me and that was all I really needed from her. I know, or I'm assuming, my therapist didn't have a childhood like mine either, but he understood me on levels I didn't previously knew existed.

◦ ◦ ◦

A great line I would use frequently with Mark was, "It's in my nature." There were—and are—traits that I developed from growing up. Living in the country with no money, no emotional affection, no effective communications, daily religious banter, and the Rosary rambled off nightly, all leading to zero connection for me and this became my norm.

So, "It's in my nature" was a great buffer that helped me avoid going deeper into the work.

Mark let me get away with that for many months until the day came when his response was, "Well, it's time to change your nature." I was dumbfounded and confused. I had no idea what that meant, and he rarely explained the process before the work.

This was a new chapter we began that day and I learned more words to explain my thinking and wiring and what was not serving me well. I didn't know that I was in charge of my own thoughts! I grew up not even knowing my body belonged to me.

It would be many more years before I could apply this insightful awareness: That we are all greatly affected by our thoughts and reactions, knowing that how we perceive the world around us determines how we feel and think.

"Each thought carries energy and thoughts are the primary forces in our life," Dr. Wayne Dyer, self-help and spiritual author, would say. *"When we change the way we look at things, things change."*

o o o

As I read through the early entries in my journal, I'm reminded about one of my first experiences of going home to Ireland one Christmas…

"I really do need to put a plan together before I go back home to Ireland for the first time in seven years. A part of me feels I will be ok, and at the same time another part of me lives in fear. Terror would be a better word.

Even when I see a man who looks like my uncle it scares me. I know it's not him, but my body gets triggered. 'I am an adult now, no one can hurt me again,' is the mantra I try to say to myself when the fear is alive. It stays in my head mostly, but sometimes traveling to the fear that sits in my tummy."

I have written, *"I hate him, I hate him, I hate him . . ."* so many times throughout the years in many different journals.

I had asked my oldest brother, Gerry, to call our uncle and ask him to stay away from my parents' home when I visited at around age twenty-five to obtain a Green Card. I stayed mostly with my sister and her husband back then, although I'd be sure to visit my parents every day.

It was also the first time I shared a part of my story with my sister and her husband. One night, my brother-in-law and I stayed up talking until 5 a.m. He was a huge support to me.

Gerry had agreed to call our uncle as I'd asked, but he was getting cold feet and decided to wait until after Christmas. That meant I had to hide for a week or stay on guard when visiting my parents.

Another brother I'd asked for help told me it was between me and our uncle. I remember feeling so alone and thinking, "Fuck everyone." I hate it so much when someone says one thing and does another.

I understand Gerry, who agreed to make the call, was scared, and didn't want to hurt our uncle's feelings, but no one understood me or my pain except Mark Fanger.

I felt I had been running my entire life. I found the courage to get sober, get honest, get real.

When I felt alone and scared, I would rely on God.

My brother must have seen the fear on my face because he eventually made the call to our uncle. So much must have been said in that short call. I felt relieved when my uncle agreed to stay away during my visit home. I was able to breathe again.

To this day I remember and appreciate my brother's support deeper than he will ever comprehend. I have thanked him many times over the years.

○ ○ ○

The pain from incest is endless, the tears always flow. I didn't feel safe being vulnerable around anyone other than Mark. I never felt comfortable. I just needed to be alone. It affected my heart, soul, and mind. The feelings I was left with were so ugly.

Each week with Mark, I found more and more courage to allow myself to be vulnerable around him. In one session, I shared a small, fragile part of me. The little kid in me, feeling naked, without a diaper. It would be many years, and many tears, in therapy before I was able to embrace and care for Little Connie the way he did from the first day he met her.

The sacred space he held for us in every session was how Little Connie and Adult Connie learned to integrate.

I hated being so needy. I hated having to discover and admit that I wasn't nearly as self-sufficient as I thought. I was operating from a place of great fear then. And yet, at some level, this was where I knew I needed to go . . . to grow.

◦ ◦ ◦

Journal Entry, from a Place of Hope and Possibility

"What we want for me . . . .

I want to feel freedom.

I want to be able to trust my own judgement.

I want to learn the difference between control and care.

I want to be free of the shame I carry deep inside of me.

I want to be free from being embarrassed about what happened to me.

I want to allow humans to care so I won't always feel abandoned and alone.

I want to learn to love myself.

I want to be able to express my anger.

I want to feel safe enough to feel vulnerable.

I want Little Connie to feel safe.

I want to be able to walk through the pain with other people.

I want to be free from the part of me that is in prison.

I want a sense of 'home' inside.

I want to feel valued as a human being.

I want to be able to address an issue as it's happening.

I want to be heard.

I want respect.

I want to be able to take criticism and still be valued and loved.

I want to feel special. 'Healthy' special.

I want to live without fear of men/people/humans.

I want to continue breaking the silence/secrets.

I want to know what my needs are and learn how to have them met.

I want to feel that it's ok to feel the vulnerability of a child and to remember I have the strength of an adult.

I want to allow myself to have feelings.

I want to have more faith so I can have less control.

I want to feel important.

I want to be able to identify my needs as they arise.

I want to be able to say 'NO' and not feel guilty.

I want to be able to take risks.

I want to be able to cherish both my masculine and feminine strengths.

I want to be able to play.

I want to nurture my soul, heart, mind, and body.

I want to accept all of me (the damaged side).

I want to connect Little Connie's pain with Big Connie.

I want to feel that I am Little Connie, that she is not another person.

I want to approve of myself, not wait for someone else's.

I want to feel the accomplishments I have made to this point.

I want to feel equal to other human beings.

I want to always respect myself.

I want to know what love is. I want to feel what love is (without sex). I also want to know what love is with sex.

I want to be able to have an adult conversation even when Little Connie wants to do something else.

I want to know when I am being manipulated.

I want to feel true happiness.

I want to feel alive just by being.

I want to like all of my body/parts.

I want to be able to not feel shame when I name a bad body part."

° ° °

The thoughts around the "wants" were easy to write but a slow, painful, grueling process to achieve. I knew it would require allowing another human into my life, which would be very challenging as the relationship blueprint I had was distorted.

August 22, 1993

I can't imagine having a normal relationship. Maybe one day.

I'm never or rarely comfortable in my own body, I constantly judge myself, I judge myself by how I look, if I look sexy or not, I always have to look in the mirror and pull my stomach in and I'm always wanting to lose a few pounds. I will continue my workouts and bike for 45 minutes and an all-body workout Tuesday after the meeting.

o o o

I hated the part of my journey where I needed to develop a healthy dependency on another human being and Dr. Fanger was the "lucky" recipient of this process.

He took an annual trip down to Cape Cod and he was smart to not give me his location, or I might have shown up on his doorstep. I'm sure his wife wouldn't have appreciated that.

It was excruciating when he would leave as I had no contact with him. He left contact information for alternate therapists in his stead, but none of them would suffice, regardless of who he or she was.

August 24,1993

"I miss Mark. He's been gone for days and will be gone for another sixteen days.

God is all I want to rely on when he's away. I feel Mark's left me, even though he's only on vacation enjoying himself and his family. A small, very small part of me, knows he needs this, but most of me resents him.

He gave me the name of another therapist if I wanted to talk with them. I don't. I don't want to talk to anyone else. Dr. Fanger is someone who can help me and listen to me. He will be back.

It's Tuesday morning at my usual AA meeting, and I'm waiting to explode. I have so much anxiety built up inside me from not being able to talk to Mark. I miss the hell out him. I want to scream right now, but it's not a good idea to do that here. I am sitting with people I don't really like or feel safe with, which may be why I don't like them. Please God, help me at least be polite."

August 25, 1993

Today on 'Sally Jesse Raphael,' the show was about inappropriate relationships. I remember so many unhealthy men that would stand in front of me, making gestures, making passes, all translating to me as 'caring,' or 'he likes me.'

I know better today, given that the first man who showed interest in me was in fact a sexual abuser. I was just a small child!

It was 'normal' that the first man that was attracted to me was older when I was a young adult. When my innocence was taken from me, it derailed me, and cut all my roots.

Back when I was being sexually violated, I still believed in Santa Claus and the Tooth Faerie.

Another abusive male would many times give me a ride home. He would stop the car many times and take my hand, place it between his legs and tell me, 'Look at what you are doing to me.' He also invited me to watch porn. I declined without ever knowing what porn was. He would also kiss me on the lips and slide his wet beer-smelling tongue in my mouth.

I would go to bed and not share it with a soul. It seemed like everyone wanted what was between my legs. Everyone.

August 26, 1993

"It's a new day. I am alive, but so is the pain of the abuse by my uncle. The mental scars from his deviant behavior sit heavily on me today. I'm looking for validation from this book The Sexual Healing Journey. I trust books, not humans. When my fear is alive, I skip the AA meeting or go and stay for 10 minutes. If it's a 'step meeting' and it's my turn to read, I get scared having to talk in front of a crowd, so I leave or go to the bathroom. I avoid adding more fear and anxiety to my existing condition.

At age twenty-four, I finally stopped biting my nails."

○ ○ ○

My cousin Barbara was someone I visited often. Her home in the Boston area was safe and she also had kids running around. Whether I was silent, crying, or laughing, I always felt accepted. She understood me and validated some of my experiences.

She was with me, not just physically, but on an emotional level, on one of my birthdays. My mom was here visiting from Ireland. It was time for me to get honest with her about her brother. It was not an easy conversation to have, but it would be more exhausting if I didn't take the opportunity to let my mom into my pain, my heart, my mind, my life.

I had no idea how she would take it or what she would say. My mom's education was limited, and her emotional understanding was lower on the scale, but I needed to do this.

It was the day of my American birthday, December 7. I celebrated my birthday on the eighth for eighteen years, until I obtained my birth certificate from the county buildings during my passport application process and discovered the actual date. Since then, I have celebrated my birthday on both days.

It was the evening before, that we had planned to have a cake at my aunt's home the next day, where my mom was staying. I would bring my own cake as I wanted to celebrate with my mom, and it had been a few years since I last saw her. I had a couple of years of therapy under my belt, as well. I got to talk with her alone that evening and I was amazed by her reaction.

Mammy cried. She told me she never knew, and that if she had, she would've "put poison in his tea." I was able to tell her it's OK, that I just wanted her to know where I'm at, and I walked away feeling understood. I felt believed and free, and I looked forward to eating the cake I was bringing to celebrate my birthday the next day.

I asked Barbara to be there also, as she was well aware of my story, or parts of it. Without hesitation, she was there for me.

I was excited driving there the next day to celebrate with my mom, her sister, and my cousin. As I walked in the door, my mom called me back to her bedroom. I was again thrilled she had something for me, or something to tell me—just me—on my birthday.

Six or seven minutes later, I walked out of that room a different person.

I had to hear my mom's new version of what my uncle did or didn't do to me. I later learned that my mom shared with her sister what I had told her about my uncle—their brother—and what he did on a regular basis to me as a child and young teen.

Her sister convinced my mom of another story, one that made me a liar, one that accused me of drinking a lot as a young teen and mistaking my uncle for other men. The "drinking a lot" was accurate, and I owned that part. But there was no mistaking who was abusing me.

I knew she wasn't reachable. My mom believed her sister over her daughter. I was numb. The joy I'd experienced the day before and the connection I thought we had just established, were ripped to shreds. I knew it would've been rude to leave at that moment, physically that is, but I had already left emotionally.

My cousin knew from the look on my face that I was not OK. She came and sat next to me. I told her in one sentence what her mother had told my mother. Barbara was not surprised but understood me and the situation from all levels.

I sat on the carpeted floor for a good part of that day as I felt very small. I lost my voice again. I was silent again, and it all translated to my mom that I was just fine.

She continued to celebrate my birthday, cut the cake like nothing happened. I got in my car later that day to go home, after a forced hug with my mom. I was hysterically crying all the way home.

I remember feeling so blessed that I never attempted to tell her about her brother when I was a child, because I thought her rejection would have been even more painful and damaging.

I cried myself to sleep and I understood then that I was newly abandoned by my mother and I felt utterly alone.

It would be ten years later before I had another conversation with my mom about my uncle. That conversation took place as we walked along Central Avenue in Needham, MA. Daddy was a few steps behind us.

When I brought the topic up again, she told me she had confronted my uncle. Unsure when she had done that, I was anxious to hear what his response was. She confidently replied, "Well, he never entered you."

That brought her much relief since it meant he wouldn't have been able to get me pregnant.

I'm sure to this day, my response to that went right over her head. "*A child doesn't know the difference between a finger and a penis.*" The rest of our walk was spent in silence.

Many times, since the age of twelve when I first got my period, my mom would utter the words, "If you ever get pregnant, I will send you away." I never knew what she meant by those words, and they went over my head.

In my home, one could display depression, anxiety, sadness, silence, or drunkenness, but so long as you weren't pregnant, nothing else seemed to impact my mother.

I remember one of the evenings at home, when I had been drinking and was depressed, and I'd locked myself in my room. There was a knock on the door and when I opened it, my mom was standing there looking helpless. The only question she had on her mind was, "Are you pregnant?" The answer was easy, "No," and she walked away.

It was many years later that I learned there actually was a place where the Irish sent their unwed, pregnant daughters.

The movie *The Magdalene Sisters* brought that to life for me after many years of living in America. As Wikipedia explains, it is a story about "institutional laundries from the eighteenth to the late twentieth centuries ostensibly to house 'fallen women,' a term used to imply female sexual promiscuity or work in prostitution. But most women entering these such laundries were unmarried mothers. In many cases these women were forced into such institutions by the powers of the Catholic Church and even family members who did not want to live with the "shame" of having a woman in their home with a baby born outside wedlock."

The last "Laundry Home," in Galway, closed in 1995.

○ ○ ○

August 30, 1993 . . . Nine Days Until Mark Returns

> *"One week from this Wednesday, 9 days from today, he returns (Yes, Mark Fanger). I can't wait, I'm so excited about it, but I don't think I will let him know how I feel. I don't want him to know the effect he has on me. I want to play it cool. I got a letter in my mail today from my oldest brother with a photo of his son, just born. I can't wait to meet him in person a few months from now . . . he looks sooo cute."*

August 31, 1993

> *"8 days to go . . . it was an ok day . . . thinking positively today about me. AA meeting helped me a lot. Seeing a few familiar faces seemed also to help."*

September 2, 1993

> *"6 days to go to see Mark, Dr. Fanger. I chaired a meeting this morning at St. Paul's . . . it was a step meeting, and*

it was on step 4. St. Paul's was a 'closed' women's AA meeting and became a staple place for me for 15–20 years.

Step 4: 'Made a searching and fearless moral inventory of ourselves.'

I heard a lot of good sobriety today. Nice ladies there . . . they may have been the same ones last week that I didn't like . . . it may be my attitude and not the actual people. God, you are so good to me."

○ ○ ○

I remember like it was yesterday, an AA meeting in Dedham, MA, a place where I felt safe, but not as a woman. It was a place I felt comfortable sitting on the steps leading into the room instead of on a chair. The chair was for grownups, and I was emotionally stuck at a very young age.

Jackson, a beautiful soul, was who I connected with the most in the meeting. He was only a few months old, and he'd smile at me from his pram, seeming to enjoy my company. He enjoyed it more than me at the time. He certainly smiled more often than I did.

Biologically I was a woman, but I didn't belong with all the other ladies. They all seemed so poised and sounded so "together" and confident. Mind you, my bar was set very low back then as to how I judged someone.

If you could talk aloud in a group, you were way ahead of me. I was not taking into consideration if what they were saying was their truth, or if they were hiding behind their voice. Looking back, I'm sure many were as wounded as me and some even more so.

I was judging their outsides by my insides.

A memory I still carry from that morning was a lady, an older, wise lady. I was stuck in my anger about one of my abusers and struggling to let go. I wanted to but I didn't know how. It was wrapped in the fibers of my being, or so I thought.

The wise lady said, "Pray for him, my dear, pray for him." I politely didn't share my thoughts with her as they would not support where she was coming from.

My exact thought was, "Yeah, I will pray . . . that a bus runs him over."

The energy I carried with me in those days was dark and heavy. I walked around in fear, even terror at times. I was jealous of women who had children, as they had, in my mind, a purpose and a reason to live. Yet some of these very same women wished they were alone like me and untethered to the responsibilities that all moms have. It was all relative.

○ ○ ○

September 3, 1993

> *"5 days to fully breathe again with Mark. Some days I feel like my head is going to explode. It hasn't yet, but the pressure and thoughts that run freely inside it feels too much some days.*
>
> *Someone I don't want to talk to is trying to reach me, someone who is not sober. Someone I don't want to come over to visit me as she is drinking. I don't want to be around active alcoholics. I may not have a choice when I'm working, but I do when I'm not. She's hoping I changed my mind.*

NO. Not this time. I have learned that 'no' is a full sentence and that I can say it without guilt. My phone is constantly ringing and I ignore it, then the doorbell is buzzing and I ignore that too. I hate that buzzing so fucking much. I want to rip it out of the wall. For now, I will put my hands over my ears until she goes away.

I knew she drove to see me, and I knew she was drinking, but I needed to take care of myself. I escaped into my shower. The door buzzer had stopped when I came out. She must have gone home. I knew I needed a meeting. I knew my friend Theresa would be there.

Another call from my drunk friend, asking about where she could find a meeting. It was an excuse to hang with me. I told her about a local meeting, not the one I was going to. I needed to put me first this time. Me, as in my sobriety.

At the meeting, Theresa and I were asked to chair. I chaired and she spoke. We went to our 'go to' place after the meeting, to Barnes and Noble in Braintree, MA. I would always go to the 'self-help' section and she went to the animal section.

She had a better connection with animals than people. We had a frozen yogurt, and I was home and in bed early. Thank you, God, for another day of sobriety."

September 4, 1993

"4 days and a big smile comes across my face."

September 5, 1993

"3 days to go . . . worked Sunday morning, went to dinner and a meeting with a sober friend. Need to work on my golf game today. I will get to the range and hit a couple of buckets of balls. Had a great talk with my brother, he is so supportive and doesn't even know it. Thank you."

September 6,1993

"Monday, Labor Day, 2 days to go . . . need to get to the gym today and a meeting."

September 7, 1993

"1 day to go . . . tomorrow I see Mark. Today I am sad, tired, lonely . . . I need help."

September 8, 1993

"The day is here. It went well. I did not like what he said about what I needed to do, but I trust him and trust he knows what I need, as I certainly don't. I cried a lot today. A lot. It's Little Connie that's sad and feels broken, broken beyond repair.

I realized he was right about what he shared with me, about my inner child. Little Connie can only be protected by Big Connie. Connie's Mammy was not able to protect her when she was a little girl. Connie is the big girl now and it's my job to take care of the little girl. More meetings, more medicine. Medicine for the mind.

It is nice to have him back. But I'm not letting him know that."

September 12, 1993

"Monday. Woke up early and smelled the fresh air and worked out with my friend Cynthia, she's got 13-month-old twins, they are adorable. We talked and listened to each other, it was a nice connection.

My distorted thoughts from being abused are always with me. I know I have to face them no matter how painful they are. God help me through today and give me the strength when I sit in front of Mark on Wednesday. I wrote a letter to my oldest brother today. I felt I needed a connection with at least one family member. I will review it with my therapist on Wednesday. I want to surrender this pain.

I want to be FREE. FREE. I want to feel free. Free from this pain. It does not belong to me.

I'm going to be a godmother on Saturday to my precious niece. She is so beautiful. I have to go to work now, but I will write more later."

September 15, 1993

"Today was a great day . . . worked out . . . at 11am I got to see Mark Fanger. I love when he smiles and laughs. He had tears in his eyes when I got through reading the letter to my brother. He reached or responded to the little me. He always knows what to say to her. He is real and genuine. Dr. Fanger is authentic. I enjoy going there every week. I know as long as I believe in the shameful thoughts, I will not get any better."

○ ○ ○

In the late fall of 1994, I was preparing to go back home to Ireland, to see my family. The courage I carried in my therapist's office would turn to ice when I eventually landed in Shannon Airport in December. I was frozen again, frozen silent.

My triggers were activated from all aspects: mentally, emotionally, and physically. I also had no sense of any spiritual connection then, and the lack of it only exacerbated the impact of the other three dimensions.

I prepared for the visit home by writing down my feelings, by acknowledging the scope of my abuse and the endless pain of it, and by connecting past events with how I felt about them in the present. In short, I was organizing my thoughts and identifying my feelings, perhaps for the very first time.

It's no wonder, then, that my journal entries at that time were a little longer, a bit more penetrating and self-aware. I was unearthing the truths that lay buried within me, like an archaeologist's dig, looking for a long-lost tomb within which some part of myself could be found and, perhaps, resurrected.

November 8, 1994

> *"Leaving for home in twenty days, and I feel more and more dissociated. I don't know what I am feeling or know the words to describe how I feel, but the pain is just as strong.*
>
> *Wednesday's session was painful . . . Little Connie was able to talk with Mark and feel safe. She shared all her wishes with him, but the adult had no wishes. This*

sharing is painful even now thinking about it, the tears are here. I need to keep being honest.

Each day is infected by my abuse issues. A day does not go by without me feeling it, a couple of hours ago I could hear a voice say, 'it was not that bad.'

How bad can it get? With what the abuse has done to my mind, my thinking is far more devastating than the actual physical touch. My thinking is so fucked up, and the pain is so great.

I had a conversation over the phone with Gerry and his wife Joy yesterday and it left me not knowing what they are doing. They are involved in some kind of 'Peace Movement' and they talked about forgiveness. I'm not there mentally and don't want to hear about that right now. There are many, many emotions that need to be dealt with before I even contemplate forgiveness, anger being one of them.

I shared with him that by the age of twelve, I did not believe my body was mine . . . and I wouldn't until I was twenty-four. I also shared with him how I hated anyone with a dick. He was silent after that sentence.

Gerry and Joy really believe in what they are doing, and it may work for them, this Peace Movement thing. For me, it will take a much longer time than a few months of therapy to get to 'forgiveness.' I don't think this will be a safe place for me. They just want me to be happy and they somehow believe that punching pillows and expressing my anger will get me there.

I have rehearsed my answers to the many questions I'm sure I will be asked upon my return home. 'Any man in your life?' will, I'm sure, be the most common. I feel so uncomfortable even thinking these thoughts . . . 'I was never the dating type.' Please, God, help me with answers to these questions when they come up, I don't want a man in my life.

I feel so sad, so sad . . . so sad . . . deep, deep inside. A little girl just went by my window at work, she smiled and waved. Maybe God is listening. Her smile was contagious, but my sadness is so heavy and I'm so exhausted.

When I awakened this morning, I didn't feel human, I wanted to stay in bed forever and have everybody leave me alone. A part of me does not want to go home. Little Connie is scared to death, she had no voice, just tears. She only wants her teddy bear in her life.

I am and always will be grateful that I met Mark. I wish it were just me and him in the world. I want to be alone, all alone. I don't feel a part of my family and sometimes I don't want to be. Even at an AA meeting recently, I wanted to be alone.

Going on 'Commitments' is good for me. I'm going to try to get a few in before I go home. I later learned that AA Commitments only happen in Massachusetts.

I feel I keep switching from Little Connie to Big Connie. I wish I had more control of that instead of being controlled by it. The pain is in Little Connie, but Big Connie is not always allowing her to express herself. If she stays buried, she will be safe. But the thought adjacent to it, is she knows it's keeping her down and that is not helping her.

She hates men and is working at a place where ninety percent of the clientele are male, and this time of the year, after Labor Day, ninety nine percent are all men. She feels safe with some of them . . . tonight, it was one person. The rest were not people I ever wanted to see again. I didn't even want to talk with them tonight. Please, God, get me through this journey.

I put together a collage . . . a lot of blackness, and a woman's body without a head . . . as this is in part how I feel inside. I also feel pretty numb right now.

Jane, a lady I sponsor, called . . . she's having a hard time and dreams are still happening to her. One of my dreams last night—or maybe nightmares would be a better description—was about a man who had his head cut off. The head came bouncing down the steps where I was standing. It never even fazed me.

Another nightmare: I was told about a neighbor of mine at home (I didn't know him) . . . he was sawing wood or a tree, and he was cutting down the branches. He turned around to where his son was standing, he sawed his son's head off and that didn't bother me either. I feel so cold to stuff.

When a lady shared about her ritual abuse at a meeting, I just sat there . . . it was like I was listening to a weather report. Sometimes I feel so cold, but the term or word Mark uses is 'dissociated.' I feel this a lot. Disconnected from myself. I feel dizzy in the morning. I also feel dizzy in the afternoon after lying down. I do enjoy working out . . . I want to feel stronger. If I get to the gym tomorrow at 5:45 am, I can do leg work out and the step class at 6:30 with Jane, one of my AA meeting friends.

Jane is a good person. I hope God watches over her. Work is slow this time of the year and there is a lot of time for thinking and writing. I don't feel real sometimes. Mark understands so much. I would love to read his notes on me. Or maybe not. He is the only one who knows me that way.

Meg, another AA friend, understands some of me as she grew up with abuse also. She was having sex at the age of seven. I could relate in part as a child doesn't know the difference between a dick and a finger. The pain is unreal. I feel like I will never heal. I feel like I need to just live in this world, my world, alone. It's a sad and lonely world and nobody is in it but me.

I am going away in 20 days from my only real link to life: Mark. I feel scared without him. 'He is only a phone call away' is what I tell myself. I can page him once a week and he told me he would be there for me in-between also, should I need to call him.

He will not keep the same time slot without paying him. I hope if he does replace my time slot, or gives it to someone else, that he doesn't tell me until I come back. Last year, when I took a few weeks off to go to the Bahamas, the time changed and it felt like it was me he was replacing, and not the 50-minute weekly meeting with him. I felt so abandoned. I don't ever want to feel that hurt again by Mark."

November 9, 1994

"Got out of work at 9:50 pm and stopped by the local shop for frosted flakes, milk and mouthwash. The sadness is so close to my eyes. Don't know why I'm sad . . . something to do with lack of money, I think. Financial insecurity and worrying about gifts and buying things. I get home and I'm filled with sadness.

There was a message from my sister on my answering machine saying she is looking forward to seeing me, her message ended with the words, 'I love you.'

I checked my mail. There was a letter from Daddy and Mammy . . . on the back of the letter was written in my dad's handwriting, "Daddy's little girl." I broke into a loud cry. I could hardly breathe, and the pain was unbearable. I longed to hear and feel these words, but there was no foundation inside me. They landed on the emptiness.

The pain was unbelievable. Writing about it is so different right now. I could hardly talk last night. I opened it and it started with, 'My Dearest little Girl, Connie.' I was unable to read another word for ten or fifteen minutes. When I got to the last sentence or paragraph, he said he would like it if I bought him a watch, as he wanted to have something from me.

I felt so overwhelmed . . . the feeling of being special was mixed in there somewhere. My daddy wanted something from me . . . this is the first time in my life that he said he would like to have something belonging to me. I didn't know what to do with the overwhelming feeling in my heart. I called Mark and he listened to me cry at the other end of the phone. He reminded me not to try to figure it out, but to just let the feelings come up . . . he stayed on the phone with me for 5 minutes and it was the best medicine. It felt so good knowing I could call him. I held my teddy bear tightly for the next 20 minutes and cried until I was so exhausted. I fell asleep.

Another restless night . . . lots of dreams, but I don't recall them. They were not clear . . . something about a bathroom. I need to rest now. I will write more later.

The feelings I had last night feel like they never happened. Today, I'm wearing a hat. I like the feeling of wearing this. I feel different, but the pain is still with me. I just need to keep it at bay at work. I have to keep it together.

The little girl in me is still silent. She wants to stay in that safe place. I just got a comment about my hat . . . I don't know him, but I know I don't like him. I want to be invisible to men. He told me I looked like I was going out riding, but without looking at him, I told him I was keeping the sun out of my eyes.

I really don't like men today. I want to hide my face when a guy comes to the window unless they are a gentleman. I do not want to make eye contact at all. If they have a certain look or energy about them, I can despise them immediately. 'Hate' is too nice of a word to describe my feelings for men. Please, God, help me through these feelings of disgust and shame, so much shame. I need my therapist to tell me it's ok, or that I don't need to talk with my uncle."

November 10, 1994

"Thoughts about Friday . . . I'm distant . . . did not make eye contact at all . . . feeling light-headed . . . felt like Thursday night didn't happen, or that it was someone else, in another time and space, or maybe it was just a dream. The same letter from my parents, that touched me profoundly, no longer appealed to me and I didn't even feel like reading it again. Feeling nothing. I did cry a little on my way home from work.

Took a shower, darkened my hair, and wore nice clothes. Went to Meg's house and took her to a meeting. Her son is becoming more and more friendly, he's a Mommy's boy.

Got to the meeting early and sat in a comfortable part of the room for me. I was asked to chair the meeting. I spoke about my experience of strength and hope, with no feeling attached to my words. I shared about seducing men, in my mind. I even shared about wanting to seduce the priest on Sunday. These words were my true thoughts. The number of times I was violated had been so overwhelming, it felt good to be the one speaking from the position of power instead of giving it away.

Even now, I feel so distant . . . miles away. Miles away from my feelings. When Ireland was mentioned today, I didn't feel excited. I feel so fucked up today, really fucked up.

Went out with Meg. Nice time and a lot of laughs . . . some tears, a lot of stories about where we ended up when drinking, what we would do to find love, attention and drugs. It was laughter with her, but we both left the shame that was attached to our stories for our therapists. We needed a break from the pain.

Friday, I came home, and I just wanted to be alone. When alone, I don't get triggered as much. I do need to return a call to Mike, another friend from the Program, as I am putting a photo album together for him and his son Max. I have the frame, just need to pick up the photos when they are ready. I feel so frozen when I'm at the park with them.

The ground is covered in leaves, I'm standing frozen as I watch Mike and Max slide together and play with the leaves. Little Connie was watching from inside, but she was frozen stiff and scared silent. I was asked to join them in the fun, but she curled up even tighter inside Big Connie.

No words would have reached her. Fun was not on her radar. She did not even feel comfortable being asked to take part. The freedom Mike and Max had was so special . . . this was a natural event for them, and it was where I captured photos of them the week prior. I was able to hide behind my lens then.

I don't have this freedom. My tears are so close, they lurk around my eyes. Most of the time, I have to stop them from flowing, as it's not safe to release them.

Max kept saying, 'Poppa, hold my hand, slide with me.' They are so happy and free together . . . nothing like a sober parent. The top layer of leaves was dry, wet at the bottom, but they didn't care. They rolled down the hill on their sides and covered one another with the dry ones. The more fun they displayed, the more trapped I felt in my own body. I want that freedom, but I am scared to death of it at the same time.

Watching Max run freely in the park, mixing with the other kids, sharing the swings and slides, was like watching a movie in part. This stuff is so painful to share with someone who does not understand. I feel enough pain already, please help me, God. God, help me through these feelings.

The feelings now are physical, not emotional, because I am not in a safe place to express them. Right now, I would do anything to be in Mark's arms. It feels like the safest place to be on this planet, as he never wants anything from me, only for me.

When he holds me each week, I am euphoric. The only real contact we had was a handshake when we first met. Writing the words 'being in his arms' is causing my body to have goosebumps . . . they are flowing through my bones as I write this. I'm so tired, so worn out. I don't know if living is what I want to keep doing. I'm so tired of feeling this way.

What the fuck is life about if you can't have the freedom to enjoy it? That freedom was taken from me. I was robbed. It was stolen by my fucking uncle. He is a fucking asshole. I feel like throwing up right now on this page, all over his name, and then hit him so hard that he can feel this same pain. Nothing I can ever do to him will give him the same experience of this pain that I carry with me every day. This belongs to him and yet I carry it. I feel so fucking angry! Fuck. Fuck! I HATE YOU! I HATE YOU!"

November 11, 1994

"I talked with Mike at length last night. I wrote him a letter explaining how I got to see and feel what was stolen from me as I watched him and his son Max playing effortlessly. It was extremely painful, but I was able to put into words what I was feeling.

Mike was a safe human, and he knew if we were to ever get intimate, I would be gone immediately afterwards. He preferred to have me as a friend, so we knew where we stood. He was in early sobriety and he appreciated my friendship. I'm building boundaries and sharing honestly how I feel and think. He welcomes this. He also needs to borrow my Higher Power as he's lacking in that area. My Higher Power was available and there for the taking any time.

Jane just called. She is in extreme pain. We are hopefully getting together tonight to talk a little . . . or a lot. Jane is in an extremely abusive relationship and can't see how to get out or maybe it's so familiar it feels normal. She may never know what a good one is supposed to feel like. Not that I do, but I know what isn't healthy. I also don't see her getting any better as long as she stays in it.

There are children in this mess also. Jane is a wonderful soul, though lost in many ways because of her childhood . . . drinking and drug use also rewired her brain.

Time to go to bed now, its 12:30 am and I'm working at 8 am."

November 12, 1994

"Got to work on time. I'm here now with my pen and paper. 17 days until my trip home, wishing Mark would come with me, sitting across from him, having him at the other end of the phone. His voice is saved on my answering machine, so I have it when I need to feel that comfort.

He returned my call very quickly. I have an image of the sandals he wears. I even bought a pair like them the last time he took a vacation. He also had a poster-size picture of Albert Einstein in his office, so I got a postcard version that I could carry in my bag. Anything to not lose the connection or anything to try to help me reconnect when I feel the deep loneliness that was doing pushups inside me.

I drew a picture of him with me curled up in his lap, a place where Little Connie imagines she would be safe. There are times when I look at the picture and feel only safety . . . other times, I feel sick at the thought of being there, and sometimes the same image can cause my body to feel butterflies. All of these could happen in the span of 30-40 minutes. So confusing. So exhausting.

The AA meeting tonight was a safe place for me to share my fear. It was safer to express this in anger. I voiced how I hated people and that I didn't care about others. It felt good to not care about what others thought of me, or how I sounded.

Saw Jane. She was in a rough place. Spoke with Danielle also, another sponsee. She is great. I committed to calling her more often.

I also gave Scottie a hug at the meeting and that felt good. He is a safe soul. Went to the gym and ran into Jack . . . his favorite topic is sex. He has many addictions."

November 13, 1994

"Talked with Mike until 1:30 am last night. I talked about all my crazy feelings.

Jack reminded me of those feelings, as he and I had talked about how painful his sexual addiction was earlier in the day. God love him. I feel so boring in that department, but I will take boring any day over the grips of Jack's addiction.

He's miles away from wanting to give up his addiction to sex. It's easy for me to think about missing a life of living on the edge during the first ten minutes of talking with him, but another twenty, thirty minutes into listening to the big picture, that yearning passes. I am months into my recovery and focusing on respecting my body and myself.

Many months earlier, I was living two lives in part. On a Wednesday morning, I attended a 9:00 am woman's AA meeting. I was in front of my therapist, Mark, at 11:00 am and later that same night, for many months, I would be with a man who was not healthy for me. I was feeling both parts of myself: the part that wants to get healthy, and the part that was abused . . . feeding both, until living from both parts stopped working. Thank God it was not the therapy that I let go.

When I stop acting out, the shame stops growing. This was not the case for Jack. It was still working for him and he needed to feed his sickness, his addiction. He was living it by talking about it.

Today I am looking forward to meeting my new nephew and brother. On a side note, my sweet friend Mike read me a bedtime story over the phone. It was very sweet and I'm sure he was a little tired of listening to my insanity. A part of me feels ashamed of liking it today. 'I am supposed to be an adult' is the chatter I am battling with. 'Only children get a story read to them.'

Sometimes I think I share too much. I will stay low key for a few days until my thoughts calm down. The part of me that enjoyed the story, wanted to curl up next to him and fall asleep safely in his arms. Big Connie was glad she was home alone.

I reached out to Meg this morning. She was so happy to hear from me, that my Little Connie was so excited. Our 'little selves' come alive when we are engaged in a dialogue. She shared with me that she doesn't feel this safe with anybody else. We were both from Ireland and we had a lot in common . . . we understood each other even when we didn't talk from our damaged places.

I feel I try very hard to be a 'good girl' for Mark. Little Connie does not always feel safe enough to smile and feel free in his office. But Big Connie knows he's the safest human on the planet in her internal and external worlds. If I had a button to push, to have her come out when I'm in his office, I would push it, but it's not that easy.

Today, Big Connie seems to be her only avenue to communicate. She talks for Little Connie. What I experience with Mark at these times, becomes a distant memory 24–48 hours later, like it was a clip from a movie and not something I was playing a main role in, either. I don't understand this today. I will ask Mark about it next time I see him, if it's still important to me.

11:25 am and I do not feel safe. I feel I do not have enough clothes on, but I'm wearing a turtleneck sweater, long johns and long pants. The only skin that's exposed are my hands and face. These feelings run much deeper than my skin.

Sick feelings come from deep inside my belly. So deep. Sometimes I do not know what's happening inside me. What is really painful at times, feels like it never happened, even if I have the evidence of stained tissues, from the sobs of my tears a few hours earlier . . . often the stains are in the form of black mascara.

I feel I am lying to myself, but it may be too painful otherwise. It's too heavy to carry it all with me. Even the shame of enjoying a fairy tale, of being ashamed of Little Connie. And I don't allow her to feel her shame. I fight so much with myself, I'm so exhausted. I know I need to let Little Connie play, but I don't know how to allow this. She is not safe. She is scared. She is frozen. She carries so much shame and guilt.

There are so many parts of me that feel fucked-up. There is a little kid like Max in me, but she is scared to breathe. Scared to be heard. I need to let her out and not be frozen. But only when it's safe. When she is not frozen, she wants to hear bedtime stories. She wants to be held, she wants to be loved, nurtured . . . she is in tears right now just hearing what Big Connie is writing.

She must be alive. I want so much for her to feel safe and secure. I believe she is at night when I am home alone. When I am with my teddy bear. At times I wish the bear were human. I don't believe I will ever trust a human like I do my bear. Mark has come very close, but it's not always as consistent as it is with my bear. Please, please, God . . . help me through this darkness, this pain. I don't feel I will even exist without it.

November 14, 1994

Feeling like a time bomb waiting to explode. Wanting to drive 100 mph in a 35-mph zone. Wanting to run people off the road as I'm screaming in my car, crying and grinding my teeth.

Went for a workout, jogged for 15 minutes, followed by a chest workout. Body toning class tomorrow. I want to jog in the morning again, so I will be in bed early tonight.

Most nights Mike enjoys the banter with me, and it puts me to sleep, so it's a win-win. Mike is a good listener. Sometimes I talk too much. I need to lighten up.

He called me first thing this morning and said he missed me and will call me later. I don't know how comfortable that makes me feel. I don't want to know he's got feelings for me. I don't want to connect with him during the day . . . at night it's ok.

Where will I start, what will I talk about in therapy tomorrow? My thoughts about masturbating? What happens with my sick thoughts? My reaction afterwards? About what my brother and his wife are doing? The pain I was feeling when I see Mike and Max playing in the leaves and how frozen I feel? Or the pain I felt when I was reading Daddy's letter? I only have 50 minutes and I need 5 hours. I don't understand what happened, what to talk about, what's most important.

I'm so overwhelmed, I need to not think about more for now.

I hope I can look at Mark while I am talking with him . . . this has been very difficult as I feel so much shame. I am still grinding my teeth.

November 15, 1994

The guy that chaired the AA meeting today looked like a schoolteacher. I was a little uncomfortable . . . he looked like he could be like the rest of the men. I loved seeing a baby at the meeting today, he was awesome. He was tired and was giving me lots of hugs. He was burying his head in my shoulder. It was so cozy, so warm. When I let him on to the ground, I crawled around after him . . . it was the highlight of my day. He loved being chased. I see him every Tuesday. Little people are so special, so important . . . and safe. I think I am going to try to catch a movie tonight. Instead of a meeting, I may tan also. My mind never stops.

God help me not to be so hard on myself. Help me give myself a little credit for staying sober despite the relentless chatter. 'God Grant me the serenity to accept the things I cannot change, courage to change the things I can and the wisdom to know the difference.'"

November 19, 1994

The time is getting closer to visit Ireland and I'm feeling more and more distant. When talking with my mom today, I was filled with frustration and anger. Not at the beginning of our conversation, but half-way through it. After talking with Mark on Friday, I was filled with anger and awareness.

Mike must have known I was hurting. He and Max brought me flowers today. It was very kind of them. I'm glad I know him most of the time.

I have not felt like writing. The abuse is such a big part of what feels like my being. I'm getting so tired from it. I will read instead. I'm captivated by a book called Universal Wound. I can relate to so much of it.

Thank you, God, for walking this day with me. Some days my mind drifts to places where I think I have more of a relationship with Mark, to be with him physically, take walks with him, to be loved by him romantically, but I know the reality is totally different. I will try to allow these thoughts to just come and go. This too shall pass.

What I really yearn for is the safety I feel in his office, sitting a few feet away from him, and it's not on a couch, but a comfortable chair. His chair is leather, and it looks far more comfortable than the one I'm sitting in, but given he's in it for hours each day, it makes sense.

Theresa and I are very different souls . . . well, our minds are anyway . . . not sure our souls are that different. Our upbringing took our minds on very different routes. But we both wanted to be living a sober life and that's what we had in common. I made the mistake of sharing deep thoughts and feelings I have about my therapist. She was disgusted and said if she ever felt that for her therapist, she would stop seeing him.

I am confused, as at some level it feels 'normal' in part to have the feelings I have for a man I see week in and week out. I learned from many of my readings there is a term called 'transference' . . . a word therapists know all about.

Theresa's doctor had her on a lot of different medications. He was a psychiatrist, but Mark was a psychotherapist. She told me I was sick to have the thoughts I have. I agree I was mentally sick, but trust me, so was she.

Just a couple of more days and I will be back in Ireland. Today a part of me is excited, and part of me is afraid . . . but the core of me will be ok. God is with me and I will take Mark with me also, metaphorically.

December 13, 1994

Today's the day . . . I will be on an Aer Lingus flight this evening. I'm outside Mark's office as I write in my car. I will be saying 'goodbye' to him soon. It's now 10:22 am and my session is at 11:00 am.

The song 'Desperado' by The Eagles is running through my head . . . a song I replayed over-and-over again when

I was high . . . and I especially like the line, 'Let somebody love you, before it's too late.' Was Mark the 'somebody'?

Today is sunny but cool. I have yet to go to Toys 'R' Us and the GNC store. I do not want to break down in front of Mark. I want to keep my shit together today.

I hope God can be with me wherever I go.

Mark often mentions the 'core Connie' and all the other aspects of her. It's like he's in my head. He reminds me of my strength. I even carry shame to say 'I have strength.' I'm ashamed to feel proud . . . 'proud' was not a feeling that was encouraged growing up, and in fact it was a put down.

I feel deeply hurt when someone is angry with me also. I feel it reaches my soul. We will not have time in the 50-minute session to touch on all of this. This session will unfold the way it's supposed to, I'm assuming. I feel I would die if Mark ever got mad at me. I will continue to go out of my way to make sure I don't upset him. Just the thought of it triggers fear and a deep cry, to the point that my body shakes. I would regress to feeling like the helpless child I was for years. I never want to feel that again as long as I live."

o o o

December 14, 1994 (Ireland)

"I am home safely now. A comfortable flight and I slept a little. Stopped in briefly to see my brother and his baby . . . he's adorable . . . the baby, that is. I will take Daddy to Mass later. I will take a break from writing and try to

just be in each experience. Sometimes I think it's easier to not always be so aware.

I feel I could sit down for one entire week and talk non-stop to Dr. Fanger.

There are so many thoughts and feelings going on inside me but I'm trying to think positive . . . but thinking positive, I'm not allowing my feelings to be expressed and I don't know how I'm feeling or why memories, remarks, or even compliments are all impacting me in a very uncomfortable way. I keep telling myself this will pass, and I tell myself I am OK, but I don't believe it.

The tears are trying to flow now, and I don't know why. Please, God, help me be able to express myself to Dr. Fanger when I return to the U.S.

Christmas is coming and I don't know in which house, or with whom, I'm going to experience it. I'm going to leave early in January to go to the Bahamas . . . please, God, so many things are happening, and I hate not sharing with anyone. I tried talking with my brother, but I was too scared, felt dirty, felt too much pain and I walked out of the house and said to him, 'Don't ever let anything happen to your baby' . . . his son was a few months old at the time.

I felt like going to bed and not waking up, ever . . . it's so hard to say how I'm feeling when I am in the middle of things. I have issues with my mom . . . they hurt so much sometimes, not knowing where or what happened to the love I am supposed to have for her . . . the abuse is amplifying in my mind . . . I carry guilt and shame and even sometimes blame.

All I feel like doing tonight is eating and eating and then throwing up. I want to curl up into a ball and roll away. My head hurts, I have been hurt by a lot of sick souls. I so don't want to be alive."

December 20, 1994

"Today was a better day . . . got quite a lot done . . . stopped by to visit with my dad and shared with him some of my thoughts and feelings. I would never be able to share anything like that with him, but for time and courage and strength resulting from the therapy, I was able to . . . through enduring the pain, I am a stronger person today and also able to share my mixed feelings with him.

A few days before Christmas, emotions are happening, sex and friendship don't go together . . . so screwed up in that area . . . food is all I want, and I can't seem to express what I'm feeling . . . please, God, help me. I feel like calling my therapist, but I don't want to call him and not have him be there . . . I will feel rejected and the 5-hour time difference doesn't help either.

AA meetings are structured differently in Ireland, but I still felt more at home with strangers in recovery than I did most days with my family of origin. Some people in AA understood me even when I didn't speak.

My trip to the Bahamas is drawing close and it will be a good distraction for me.

It will be with people I know but have not really socialized with before. They like to drink, and smoke weed, and I am in early sobriety, and in part alone. This aloneness is not as painful as the aloneness I feel when I am around my family."

◦ ◦ ◦

Rose Island was so beautiful. It's a small island off the Bahamas. My boss invited me and some coworkers to spend twenty-one days on the island. It was paradise.

There were lime and lemon trees as I walked down the steep stone steps to the beach each morning. I became good friends with Columbus and Sable, the two dogs that came with the rental home. I took photos of the sunrise. I felt at peace while on that island.

We accidentally sank the boat we rented and were not allowed to rent another boat. The island was small, and word got out!

Some mornings I went back to bed after catching the sunrise, and I wrote daily in my journal. I wrote to Mark like I was talking to him.

There was a private place on the beach where I could be by myself.

One morning I was scared. I was lying on my beach chair in a small inlet on the private beach, eyes closed, and I felt the energy of someone near me.

My eyes opened to see a big black guy with his arms crossed in front of his chest staring at me. He scared me. I told him I wanted to be alone, repeating, "Leave me alone" many times. I had no idea if he understood me or not. He was wearing a thong, just enough material to cover his private parts. As I got up to leave, he ran into the woods.

His footprints were all around my chair like he was walking around in circles and I felt terrified, but I think I scared him, too. He uttered a few words, but I didn't understand him.

After a walk later that day, my head felt like it was trapped in a vice. It was an early night, and I went to bed at 8:45.

It was quiet most mornings, as the other guests were hungover or slept late. I wanted a tan and to get a slimmer body; I was on a mission to lose weight. Many times, I wished I was sitting in Mark's office.

The Serenity Prayer was something I said often to myself, for strength and for peace of mind, to feel at ease, knowing my connection with God had become solid: *"God, grant me the serenity to accept the things I cannot change, courage to change the things I can, and the wisdom to know the difference."*

I wrote on day twelve, "*This trip had many highs and many lows. It was a cloudy day and my mood is not good. I want to be nowhere . . . not here . . . not anywhere.*

I can't concentrate on a movie. I lose interest. I can't stand having someone look over my shoulder constantly. Even having someone sit too close to me is uncomfortable."

One morning I sent a message in a bottle, wishing someone who found it a Happy Valentine's Day!

That was the highlight of my Valentine's Day.

Day 14

> *"Very bad weather here . . . stormy, windy, thunder and lightning all day!*
>
> *It's now midnight and I'm going to bed . . . please, God, help me grow while I sleep!*

Tomorrow is another day. I hope I eat less tomorrow."

Day 16

> *"5 days left on Rose Island . . . today I woke up and there are sun blisters on my face . . . too much sun yesterday.*
>
> *I miss my smooth skin. I promise to not soak under the sun again if these blisters go away."*

My dreams were endless during this time. Each occurred to teach me something . . . I was unsure what the "something" was.

> *"Mark was in my dreams . . .*
>
> *Some of my dreams were about people dying. I was crying a lot in my dreams.*
>
> *It felt so good to wake up from the heavy dreams.*
>
> *There are many magical moments here when I think about sleeping under the stars.*
>
> *Sunshine really helps my mood. I wish I could swim, but that's also a scary thought.*
>
> *It's coming time to go back to Boston. I have many memories that I will take back with me. I will continue to get on my knees and ask for help. I need to learn how 'to be' in this world without booze and drugs.*
>
> *Keeping a journal during the last week of the vacation has kept me grounded, as there was no AA meeting and most of the people in the house loved booze and weed. 'Pinky' was a boat driver who used to take us inland for*

groceries. I was able to find some peace in the silence and beautiful ocean.

I asked God daily to help me heal and grow!"

◦ ◦ ◦

At this time, with the trips back home to Ireland and the one to the Bahamas behind me, the grueling journey of more therapy work lay ahead.

I'm remembering a phrase from Mark when the work ahead seemed difficult: "Fasten your seatbelt."

February 8, 1995

"I'm in a real good space . . . I went to see Mark today which always helps. I don't feel alone with him . . . I hope I can carry this good feeling with me. I was able to go a little deeper emotionally today with him . . . it is a very slow process . . . very slow.

I always ask God to give me what I can handle and today it was a part of me. I prayed that if I shared with Mark that the lonely, scared girl inside me is afraid because he is a man, and I was afraid she would be sent elsewhere, that Mark would not want to work with me . . . I need, she needs, to be reassured that no matter what I share with him, we will not be sent away.

I felt I was at times a bother to him and was scared that he would send me away to someone else . . . Little Connie needed to let him into her lonely space . . . she needed to introduce herself to Mark. I needed to let her out slowly and gently . . . she needs to know she's 100% safe, as she knows she will not feel that way often . . . but if the adult can hold onto the knowing, it would be safer.

She needs to know she will be protected as the work ahead will not feel safe or good . . . it's 50 minutes once a week.

Sometime this week I'm going to let Little Connie listen to lullaby music, and maybe I will be able to write about her . . . and by next week, Mark may be able to talk with her directly. They need to meet each other . . . she will be able to meet a nice man, a man that will not abuse her or hurt her. Little Connie, please come out soon . . . please, God, give us a voice so we can help each other together through this time. We'll be ok.

At one point, Mark knew I needed more than 50 minutes once a week . . . he knew I needed to learn to depend on someone, to learn what it was like to have someone there when I needed them.

He came up with a plan that I'd check in with him twice a week over the phone, in addition to our session.

At one point he dropped one of the check-ins and again I felt he was getting tired of dealing with me. I felt rejected and a bother to him, with now only being allowed to check-in once a week . . . he was getting rid of me slowly . . . rejection was the top layer of my skin."

February 9, 1995

"It was my parents' 36th wedding anniversary. I called home and brought up my abuse to my mom. My mom says she believes me, but there was no foundation for these words to land within me. I need to slow down, maybe go

to bed. Please, God, help me have the strength to read this to Mark tomorrow."

February 15, 1995

"Going to see Mark again tomorrow. I still wish sometimes that he was attracted to me sexually and that way I'd know he would really care about me. But I feel a little different right now . . . I want him to get to know the lonely Connie, the one that is living in a dark hole, alone and sad. I want to let him in and when I think about letting him in, the only 'in' I know is sexual.

The 'in' that I know is necessary for the healing to evolve, is 'in' to my pain and 'in' to my fears . . . 'in' to my abandonment . . . and as I write this, that's where I know the terror and trauma lie within me. Please, God, give me the courage to share all this with him tomorrow. The part of me that is not afraid, the part of me that wants to seduce him, is not real . . . so many racing thoughts, all at the same time.

I have fantasies that I'm afraid to share with him as I know I will be rejected, and I will feel victimized all over again. I don't want to be touched sexually, but I want him to want me like the abusers wanted me. There is also a part of me that wants to curl up in a ball, fully clothed, and live under his arm, his wing . . . a feeling of safety and protection always.

I love to feel safe. When I look at him, I usually want to cry I feel so sad. I want him to do something with the pain he knows that I am feeling, but all he does is just sit there and not take it. If I don't make eye contact with him, it doesn't feel so painful. How can he just sit there and look at someone in so much pain and not do anything?

I guess I want to be comforted in his arms and feel safe . . . I want him to take the pain away, just take it. It hurts to look at him. There is also a part of me that feels he does not care, that he sees people like me all the time, and I'm just another patient. Just another 50-minute patient and that hurts also.

Mark is so professional, with unshakeable boundaries, and I learned a lot from those boundaries. I did not know what the word 'boundaries' meant, until I read one of John Bradshaw's books, Healing the Shame that Binds You.

I don't want to be violated anymore. I'm so glad my therapist is who he is . . . I owe him so much. I think I'm ready for growth . . . sometimes I talk too much about myself . . . I want to learn a new way of living with boundaries."

February 17, 1995

"Sitting here again on a Friday night at an AA meeting, I wanted to get better . . . I've been doing really good . . . it may be related to going away and burying my issues real deep. I don't feel the pain of it today. I'm trying to focus on what Oprah shared about learning how to not be a victim . . . I am tired of the pain that I'm feeling. I want to be free of this shit . . . I want my freedom to make mistakes, freedom to learn and live, freedom . . . to care about freedom, freedom, freedom.

All I want is my freedom.

I am eager to learn about Connie. I'm going for a complete physical. I'm trying to accept the damage and learn to heal it and live the life that God had intended me to live.

I've had so much of my life taken. I don't want another single person to take another hour from me . . . it is important to feel my pain as it is coming up, not bury it with food.

Mark has meant so much to me during my recovery . . . he is my beacon, my light, and believes I am ready for group therapy. I don't know what it would be like in a room with other people . . . what will my goals be? I do need to make a list of my goals, Connie's goals.

Whenever the conversation came up about group therapy, which was often, I'd feel that Mark was tired of dealing with me alone. But, I also learned over the early years that when Mark made a suggestion like this, it was for my own good.

It would be 4 years into my individual therapy that I finally agreed reluctantly. I had no idea what I was signing up for, and if I did, I may not have agreed . . .

But, it was exactly what I needed."

o o o

Journal Entry, 1996:

"I don't feel like I am heard or understood anymore . . . today he was so mean.

Dr. Fanger put me in with a big crowd, but God knows you still feel lonely. I know what it's like to be lonely and I feel I have been alone my entire fucking life . . . fuck you, fuck you—he was no longer a safe place for me to fall.

What do we do now? Where do we go? Who do we turn to for help? I don't feel like Mark can help me. His approach on Wednesday didn't work and when he asked what I needed from him, I didn't know the answer . . . . my only reply to him was "Nothing" . . . I felt so alone, and broken, broken beyond repair. He did not agree.

I do know now, but the trust between us was shattered in my mind, fear was taking over . . . it was no longer 'Mark and me' . . . now I had to share him.

I don't feel like he can help me anymore and I don't know if I can help me anymore. This was the lowest—or one of the lowest—moments I experienced with Mark."

○ ○ ○

My perception was completely distorted at this time.

I had done some amazing work and healing with Mark in individual therapy, and he knew I needed more, more than what he could give me, more than what I could accomplish with him alone. I needed to work on interpersonal relationships and not just one-on-one.

I didn't understand this and at the time, I felt like he was tossing me aside, abandoning me to the notion of group therapy, with people other than myself and Mark alone. I felt that he was tired of dealing with me on my own and wanted to throw me into a pack of wolves.

One of the wolves was "Carla," and she scared me the most.

She appeared big and could be very mean to my adult. She was often mad at me and tried to lecture me. Her "Priscilla"—an alter self—is evil and I don't think part of her cares about humans and that really scared me. Priscilla may be Carla's protector, but she's got no care or remorse for others. She was raised in the home of an undertaker and shared the home with dead bodies.

Mark had thrown me into the crowd, and I wanted to be alone. I wanted to have the same comfortable feelings that I have had with him, but the energy in that room shifted when the other humans entered it.

I understand today that the work I needed to do could not be accomplished in a one-on-one setting. I needed to heal at a deeper level.

Journal Entry, 1996:

> *"I don't like how Mark talks to me in group . . . I feel disappointed. I want him for myself. I don't like to share him. I don't hate him, but group therapy is not where I want to be on a Thursday night (our group therapy was held on Thursday nights).*
>
> *The thoughts still come, they are stuck in my head, they are very loud, and they are confusing. I have group therapy today and I'm not looking forward to it. I don't even care about the people.*
>
> *I have zero interest, care, empathy, compassion or love for these group members. This is a very comfortable place for me to be as I don't know how to feel and express any other emotions.*

Mark Fanger does not know everything . . . he betrayed me, he hurt me more than words can say, and he wants to move past it. The day before, he compared me to the other members of the group . . . I was crushed and devastated because I was no longer special. Why couldn't he see the pain even if I didn't voice it? How could he be so blind? I guess he can't read my mind. I don't know if his apology would mean anything to me . . . it's too late. I feel I need to move on.

Today I do not like Mark, and 'Little Connie' will not trust him and can't trust. Without trust, we can't do the work. Do I want to build the trust back? Why? I need to take care of me anyway. I am not going to allow my little person to get that close to him again. I do want to tell him how much it hurts. I don't like when he compares me with the other people. I want to be special to him. I actually want to be his only client, which I know would not pay the mortgage . . . in fact, I don't even think it would pay the electricity bill. I don't like sharing him.

What do you think, Little Connie? What do you think of Mark? I'm no longer safe, or no longer feel safe".

I sat next to the door the next four years in case I had to exit quickly from these other humans, male and female.

They all had many hurt parts that they carried with them.

Hurt people hurt others.

° ° °

They were polite the first few sessions, but that would change. It took a good year or longer for my attitude to change. I sat there with my arms folded for protection and my "mental" gun loaded, ready to shoot at anyone that would address me in a nice way or a painful way. Everything hurt.

I had no foundation inside me for relationships, except with Mark. I carried myself well and I could always look good on the outside. You could dress me up and I would fit in anywhere. But rarely did I feel how I looked on the outside.

My clothing and high heels protected me, like a mask, or a suit of armor. I was called a bitch and a snob, which landed nicely on me . . . it kept me distant from them. I was more comfortable with being a bitch than a loving, kind person.

I was terrified, terrified of humans. Even Mark was no longer safe when he was leading the group. He wasn't mine anymore. I didn't feel he cared about me and all the others in the group, so I took a step back every Thursday night, knowing the following Wednesday at 11 a.m. I would have him to myself again for fifty minutes.

Today I know my heart holds love for many people all at the same time, a concept that was very foreign to me back then.

Group therapy was not easy, unlike AA, where there was often a theme or the chairperson would get the meeting started. Most times, group would start with silence. I hated silence, especially silence when other people were present. It was like the home I grew up in . . . no one talking to one another.

The silence was deafening.

As my anxiety rose, it took everything I had to keep it all inside. It did not feel safe to breathe fully with other humans. I used to rely on a quote I once heard: "Don't let them see you sweat, as they will kick you when you are down" . . . and one of the group members did exactly that, on more than one occasion.

Eventually, when I did allow myself to be vulnerable, one of the male members would always throw something up in my face about some previous sessions, and he could not allow me to be present in the moment. Mark didn't help me either. He just sat in silence. This same guy was terrified of my "bitch side," which I took pleasure in. I felt powerful on those evenings when I wasn't vulnerable.

My truth today about this is the very opposite . . . it's powerful to be vulnerable, and I know the stubborn "bitch side" derives from a place of fear. Each session was from 6 to 7:45 p.m. It was in the same room as I did my private sessions, but it was a different energy.

I longed for the session in group to be done and wished I could sit with Mark alone for hours. I remember fantasizing about moving in with him . . . I was smiling as I was telling him this. I told him I would be so quiet he would not even know I was there. He smiled. We both knew being in his presence was where I felt the safest on this planet.

Mark and I made a deal about bringing "Little Connie" to group and not hiding behind him to feel safe. I hid behind my chair. I needed to be around the group because I was scared to be alone and scared that I needed a subgroup, with people I could feel were on the same page as me.

I used to sit near the door during our private sessions and next to him in group therapy. I did two four-year stints of group therapy.

Really, there is no amount of individual therapy that would teach me what I learned in group therapy. Despite Mark's explanation of group therapy, I think I thought about the idea for two years before I made that commitment.

He would revisit this periodically and he always got the same stubborn answer from me, "No way, you are not going to throw me into a pack of wolves."

There were many times I felt like they were a pack of wolves. Some Thursday nights I got to experience exactly why he wanted me there. I needed to learn how to have relationships with other human beings and not just the one-sided relationship that individual therapy provides. It was not a fun experience, but I would not be as integrated and emotionally evolved today without these painful lessons.

It may have been another year or two, maybe even three, before I thanked Dr. Fanger. He smiled as though he was thinking, "I told you so," but he didn't speak it. He knew my fear, he knew my limits, he knew when to push me, and he knew when *not* to push me. Mark knew me better than myself.

I used to tell him how miserable I was each week and the only time I felt good was during the fifty minutes sitting in front of him every Wednesday morning. He suggested one day, "Why don't you be miserable for the fifty minutes while you're here and maybe the rest of your week might feel better?" He often said things to me that didn't always make sense, but I did it anyway and I under-stood exactly what he was saying.

It was like living two different lives for a period of time, learning a new language in a way. It was a language that I was never exposed to before. I'd never even know anyone who had done therapy. But I knew at some level it was what I needed.

My first four-year group stint ended when I decided to go to massage school, a one-year, part-time curriculum. One of the classes fell on a Thursday night.

The group was not happy with me. The respectful and meaningful way to terminate group therapy would ordinarily be a four- to five-week process. I told them the week before I left.

A vivid memory from that last night in group, was one of the members with whom I never had a connection. She said to me, "I finally know what my work would be with you, as you remind me of my selfish mother." I quietly thought to myself, "I'm glad I'm not going to be your punching bag."

Another way of describing group therapy is getting to relive our family of origin through the different members of the group. Each member carries their own neuroses from their childhood, which eventually get exposed in the group, triggering one another's unhealed parts.

A focused, committed, boundary-driven therapist like Mark is able to guide and support the members through that journey.

○ ○ ○

My second four-year stint in group therapy started out a little easier, as I knew what to expect. But I still had many challenges ahead with new wolves:

"Peter" - The part that scared me about Peter, was that he got frustrated with me and thought I was full of shit. Sometimes that scared me away.

"Scott" - I was fearful of him wanting to get close, and it helped that he had a daughter. I was less fearful, but still scared.

"Stephanie" - I had no thoughts about her and I didn't know her and she didn't know anything about me. She didn't last long enough in the group to be known. The work that transpires in group therapy is not for thin-skinned people.

"Dan" - He was a gay male in his sixties but was raised Catholic and was always too religious to act on it.

"John" - He was a family guy, reserved, mostly kind, and he carried his pain deep inside.

"Rhonda" - She had multiple personalities. None of them happy.

Journal Entry, February 28, 2004:

> *"Group went very well. Like all new relationships, everyone tries to be on their best behavior in the first few gatherings, but eventually, their neuroses follow, as did my own.*
>
> *Stephanie was out and will be out for two weeks total. I was amazed how I felt with the original gang and more amazed that I shared my feelings with them. I felt like I was with my family and that it should be just us and no one else. This feeling didn't last very long . . . not that I know what a 'family feeling' feels like but it was what I imagined it to be, since we all communicated with one another effortlessly that night.*
>
> *The most intense time was during the Fall, when we'd spend one weekend together in a nice, secluded home on the Cape with our therapist. The weekend began at 8:00 pm sharp, Friday night, for a 2-hour session. Saturday, we had three 2-hour sessions with a break in between. We ended Sunday morning with another 2-hour session.*

We had limited rooms, so often we were expected to share rooms. Once, in the 8 years, I shared a room . . . for the other 7 years I opted for the couch.

The one time I did share a room—that I shared with Rhonda—it was a very different experience. My Little Connie got to play with all her inner children. It was refreshing to experience that Rhonda did have some happy parts deep within her in the form of little children.

I was hesitant about a story I wanted to share with Mark one day in individual therapy. I wanted to make it sound right and I wanted it to be the entire truth. Mark gave me the freedom to share it and if I wanted to add to it or take it back later, he'd let me. There was no right or wrong way of being in his office, all of me was welcome to every session.

Many times, he would ask the adult me to wait in the car, as 'she' wanted to be the voice for the unhealed parts. To heal, the 'little me' needed to be heard and to claim her own space on this planet.

Most of the time, the little kid in me was scared . . . scared silent. Mark was a tall giant in Little Connie's eyes, but that part of me only got to have a voice, or say, after many months into therapy.

Her favorite place was in silence. It was familiar, not comfortable. It was scary, not safe . . . but, it was where Little Connie hid inside for many years. Mark was the first safe man who wanted to hear her, wanted her to have a voice, wanted to metaphorically hold and protect me.

He did all of that from across the room with his words, his compassion, his kindness, and—more than anything—his relentless belief that I would heal and I have to add, it helped to know he would be in that room, in that chair. Every Wednesday at 11am was for ME.

He seemed very old when I started my journey. I told him a few years in, he was getting younger. He smiled and reminded me it was my perception that was changing as he was not getting younger. I had to agree. As I aged, he stayed the same. Now I think I am the age he was then when we first started our journey together. Time does not stand still.

There was very little of me in therapy today and as soon as I voiced that, it allowed the rest of me to show up. Mark wanted to know if I wanted to be there. I said with tears in my eyes, 'I want to stay here all day.'

I wanted things to be different . . . dim the lights, leave a part of me with him today. His words didn't reach me. I know he cares. I know he doesn't think less of me. I know in my head, but he didn't reach my heart or soul.

Please, God, help me."

o o o

I had a very brief relationship with an angry guy named Howard and that experience led me to Dr. Neil Carter, a couple's therapist. The first two sessions we had were clearly too much work for Howard, but I knew I had work to do with Dr. Carter.

I didn't know at the time what work we needed to do, but I felt compelled to continue seeing him. The relationship with Howard ended quickly, but my connection with Dr. Carter evolved into an amazing therapeutic journey that lasted one year.

Dr. Carter was in his late sixties, early seventies. His wife worked in the same office. The forty-five-minute drive south every Friday evening was so worth it. Each session would start with him saying, "How're you doing, Good Heart?"

A few minutes into each session, he'd take a moment and look out the window to make sure his wife got into her car safely. He knew the sound of her door closing as she exited the building. He was nothing like Dr. Fanger. But his non-traditional approach was exactly what I needed.

Most of our sessions involved sitting on the floor with me in his arms. I felt it was 100 percent safe and appropriate, precisely what I needed to feel, as it was something I never experienced as a child. Most sessions I sobbed like a three-year-old, with no stories attached to the tears, just a deep, deep sadness. I continued to sob for many weeks in his arms.

After he saw I was healing from our sessions on the floor, he wanted to teach me how to nurture myself and reclaim that little girl I left in Ireland. We sat on the floor and created an imaginary ring. There were three different parts of me: my spiritual self, my adult self, and my emotional self. He was always there when I needed guidance.

Over many weeks, each Friday night, it was always with the same warm start, "How ya' doing, Good Heart?" It was always welcomed with a smile!

My eyes could be opened or closed for this process and I opted for closed, as the images in my mind became stronger when closed. It would take weeks before seeing results. The process involved guiding the three different parts of myself along a journey back to Ireland to reclaim Little Connie.

It was fascinating when "we," all three parts of me, would surround Little Connie, who stood quietly in her pink "cot," a wooden crib I remembered from my early childhood.

My dad made it for me. It sat in the middle of the main room floor with a bicycle tube attached to both sides, acting as a swing . . . it had a pink Bambi-like sticker on one side of the cot with some of its face scratched off. This was the image that appeared vividly as I thought about Little Connie.

As we circled around her in the cot, Dr. Carter guided me to put my hands out to pick her up. She seemed frozen and didn't know how to respond to out-stretched arms. Each week the results were similar. Little Connie didn't seem to know how to be nurtured.

One of the weeks, Dr. Carter said, "Just pick her up."

She sat with ease on my right hip. He asked, "What did you like to do as a kid?" I quickly responded with, "Jump on the bed." He suggested I drag the bed outside and jump on it with her! We did. She still didn't smile but looked more alive.

Eventually it was time to take her to America with us (me). We literally visualized driving on the left side of the road, with Little Connie safely strapped into her car seat. We boarded an Aer Lingus plane to Logan Airport, and it was time to take her home.

One of the other tools Dr. Carter suggested, was to buy a doll that would represent Little Connie. The Cabbage Patch dolls were popular at the time and one of them became Little Connie.

I made sure she was wrapped in a warm, clean blanket daily and left in a safe place while I was not home. I would also talk with her like she was my baby and I even took her to bed with me at times so she could feel safe and loved.

I clearly remember a day when I was saying goodbye to her as I left for work. As I walked over the threshold of the door, I could hear a little voice asking, "Where are you going? Please come back!"

It was so beautiful! I returned and sat with the Cabbage Patch doll, my little self, and told her, "I will be back later. I have to go to work." She finally started to trust me. It was an amazing experience that I didn't share with Mark, as his style of therapy was very different, and I didn't think he would approve.

There was no amount of talk therapy that would have given me the insight and the feeling of what it was like to be held as a child, which I was starved for. I also would never have been able to accomplish what I did with Neil, in the same way with Mark. I needed both therapists, both approaches.

Dr. Carter's and my work ended when we felt it was time to move on. I am forever grateful to him. I'm sure his body has transitioned by now, but his soul lives on within me.

Thank you, Dr. Neil Carter, thank you!

FIRST MEANINGFUL RELATIONSHIP

Five years into my recovery, another troubled dimension of my life reared its ugly head, in the form of bulimia.

It was also when I entered my first meaningful relationship.

Gianni was a good soul, separated from a wife, and on a path to divorce. He knew far more than me about relationships, so the next five years had many ups and downs for me.

Given what my body had been through, with inappropriate touching for so many years, I really didn't know how to respond to safe, mature, consensual touch. It was a very confusing period of my life and I'm sure it was confusing for him also.

I look back now and if I were to analyze it, I would say yes, it was a five-year relationship. We dated for six months, but then I spent the next four and a half years on a mission trying to change him. An impossible chore and an unfair task.

The man I was trying to change was a good soul, but also emotionally constipated. A very familiar energy for me to be around. So, in hindsight, instead of wanting my mom to be different, I focused on him. Gianni had no idea what thoughts were going on between my ears and never asked. Smart on his part, and I say that with a smile today.

He was not dating other women when we met, and I thought or assumed it was going to be a monogamous relationship. Then, eight months into the relationship, I learned he'd been on at least one overnight with another female.

Whatever trust I thought I might have been developing for him—the first person I wanted to trust after Mark Fanger—was shattered.

I know many souls can forgive and act like this was nothing. I'm just not one of them. It would take another three years for me to step into my own integrity, my own truth, and say goodbye to Gianni with zero resentment. I knew it was over for me once I fully accepted him for who he was. I no longer wanted to change him.

I learned a lot about myself during those five years. I learned that I was capable of love. I was capable of honesty. I was capable of being loyal. I was trustworthy.

I also learned it's probably not a good idea to get involved with a man who hasn't been removed at least a year or two from his previous relationship. There's the healing, growth, forgiveness, and maturity that need to occur to be ready to be fully involved in another relationship. None of this had happened in my situation.

We still managed to have some wonderful days and nights, moments together in nice restaurants, and trips to Nantucket. The highlight was when we decided to buy a Golden Retriever.

I have never seen so many beautiful furballs in my life as I did when these Golden Retriever puppies waddled up to me. I remember like it was yesterday. One of them bumbled over to me and I knew this was the little guy we were taking home.

He picked me.

We returned a few weeks later to take our boy, Zak, home.

I reassured him as he sat on my lap in the front seat, whimpering a bit, that he was going to be OK. I cuddled and stroked the furball until he finally drifted off to sleep.

I do believe over the next four years Zak may have been the real reason why I stayed in the relationship. He was so filled with love, energy, enthusiasm, and a zest for life that I had never known a dog could possess.

Growing up I would see dogs neglected and abused—mostly in the form of being drowned—but I never felt what I felt for this little guy. I still remember many nights sitting on the stairs. I would be crying over the emptiness and disconnect I felt in the relationship with Gianni, and he would lick my tears.

I also know how special he felt in my company and my energy. He was so loved. The day I knew, despite my love for him, that the journey with his "dad" had ended, I needed to say goodbye.

Gianni and I had brought one another as far as we were supposed to.

We had a wonderful dog-walker. I knew the time she came by every day and the path they walked. On many days over the next six months or year, I would stalk Zak and his walker. A few times I got out of my car and just smiled at Zak and hugged him to feel his excitement one more time. He never forgot me, and the feeling was mutual. That is still how I feel today, even when I'm sure he's in doggy Heaven.

° ° °

I knew my bulimia stemmed from not knowing how to handle different emotions, even the good ones, or I might even say, "especially the good ones."

But as always, when I brought this new piece of information to my therapist Mark, he gave me a different perspective. He gave me a choice, as he often did. It was, "I can send you to a behavioral therapist, or we can continue dealing with the underlying causes."

That was an easy answer for me. I wasn't interested in seeing a different therapist and trusted that Mark believed that by doing the work, we'd discover the underlying causes triggering the bulimia.

I didn't always want to do the homework he suggested, which was to acknowledge and write down the feelings I was having prior to wanting to overeat and purge. Purging would give me that feeling of emptiness, which was clearly masking other uncomfortable feelings, and I felt out of control.

Food seemed to be the only thing I could control.

Within a year, I got to live what Mark suggested would happen if I did my work. As I continued to clear out the pain, the desire to self-destruct diminished.

He was right, as he often was.

° ° °

The demise of my relationship with Gianni was a direct result of the group therapy that allowed me to engage with other humans.

There, we learned to communicate effectively, express our feelings, understand our emotions, and have them validated. That was not something Gianni and I were ever able to achieve.

It also didn't help that three years into our five-year stint, he decided he needed a break from us to "find himself," as he claimed.

Unless he was lost on a golf course, there was no chance of his finding himself.

I asked if he wanted to stay committed. He immediately answered, "No, we'll go our separate ways."

As I pulled out of his driveway, the tears flowed down my cheek and the feeling of abandonment was reignited like a lit match in a room filled with gasoline.

ANOTHER ADDICTION

Three months alone was what I thought I was about to experience. Instead, it was three months of excitement, flowers, phones calls, excessive texting, and the highs from the addiction of love.

I was Cliff's drug, and he was mine.

Thank God his addiction was stronger than mine. I had done some healing around addiction, but not this type of addiction.

o o o

It was three years into my previous relationship, despite having lost my trust for Gianni a year and a half earlier, when I wanted to have a conversation with him: "So, where are we going with our relationship?"

The script was to get married, have kids, and live happily ever after. Not sure whose script that was, but it wasn't ours.

I was shocked and saddened that he wanted time alone. He clearly had thought about it, as it flowed so easily out of his mouth. "I want three months to myself."

I didn't let him see how I felt. I was holding back my tears until I was alone in my car. Not only did he want this time to himself, but he also wanted us to both have the freedom to see other people.

This was the last thing on my mind.

o o o

I had a friend/acquaintance back then, a man I enjoyed innocently flirting with. He, too, was in a relationship and he frequented my place of work.

When he learned I was free, he was delighted to tell me he'd broken up with his long-term relationship a few months earlier. I didn't feel free. I felt lost and sad, but that was about to change. Cliff was about to take me on a life-changing ride.

It started with a simple lunch where I whined and vented about all that I was missing in my now-broken relationship. Gianni was not romantic, never sent me flowers, didn't give me many compliments, never checked in during the day . . . I went on and on.

I didn't know Cliff's emotional or mental state, or how toxic he was, or how much he represented my abusers, or the pain that would come with this newfound excitement.

The next three months were filled with flowers delivered twice a week, so many texts I could hardly keep up with them, and a constant smile on my face.

I had no idea how much I was dying inside from the loss of my last relationship—the one with Zak's dad—or how much life I had inside me yet to live. It felt amazing, but I also knew there was an unhealthy aspect to it.

If something is too good to be true, it probably is.

My morning, noon, and night were filled with messages from Cliff: compliments, questions, sweet words. Everything I was yearning for and more. I drank it all in and I wanted more.

But, just like drinking alcohol, one drink was too many and a thousand weren't enough.

Being addicted to something is one thing. But being addicted to someone with a heartbeat was very different.

He knew I was hooked. I was his next victim. I walked into his world with open arms, a willing participant. I now had more life lessons to learn and these were deep rooted.

The three months passed, and Gianni assumed he could just pick me up where he dropped me off.

I was a changed person. I had awakened in ways that would never allow me to go back to sleep; I wanted to stay awake.

Gianni had a dozen red roses in his car for me when he picked me up for dinner. I had received so many flowers the previous three months, that these roses had very little effect on me. I did love Gianni, but the excitement I had now was for Cliff.

In part, it felt like going back to prison, or going into a dark room. Gianni was a good soul. I loved the way he had great plans for us, but he didn't seem to think I should have been part of making decisions about us.

His intentions were good. I should have been thrilled that he wanted to be back together, to ease the pain I felt with the loss, but that feeling was not there.

I felt depressed. I only had feelings for Cliff, even as I lay next to Gianni. I felt a thousand miles away from him, but he didn't seem to notice. Another of my many complaints.

I was hoping it would pass and that I would feel what I felt for him three months earlier. This was not to happen.

I wanted us to work. I was in love with his potential. We had three years together. So I reasoned that was enough to try to make it work.

Cliff assumed I would never share information about our time together. He lived and took pride in being with other guys' ladies. His thrills came from the secrets he carried, like when he was in the same room as his male friends and knew he'd slept with their wife or girlfriend.

He was a sick soul.

Cliff became friends with Gianni as they both frequented the same driving range to work on their golf game. He even accepted an invitation to play golf with Gianni, an invitation he would never have gotten if Gianni knew about the fun we had for the few months during our breakup.

Cliff told me once he was not a good guy, but I didn't want to believe him. Later I would see that his actions followed his words.

Cliff would go out of his way to practice his golf game next to Gianni, making sure I watched. He never thought I would share our secret with Gianni. I was someone who carried many, many secrets from my childhood. This secret I could not keep.

I needed to be true to myself. I knew if I was going to give us a chance at redeveloping our relationship, Gianni needed to know the truth of what I'd been doing and who I was with during the three months he was enjoying his freedom.

I worked hard at trying to re-establish what I yearned for with Gianni for another year and a half or so. The idea of not being around to see Zak daily was heartbreaking. I loved that boy so much.

I was never able to feel the same love for Gianni again. I needed to learn a new normal. I was not happy.

When I look honestly at those five years together, there was much I needed to learn and I believe he needed to learn, as well. Even though I learned he had a sexual encounter a year and a half in, and there may have been more than one, that single time was enough for me to justify leaving.

I had learned to trust him until he violated that trust. I never trusted him again after that day. I second-guessed all his business dinner meetings and I didn't trust him when he was on his boys' weekends, which were three to four times a year or more. It was a heaviness I carried in every pocket.

The good news was that I was growing, changing, and evolving weekly in both individual and group therapy. I knew that Cliff was not healthy, and each time I would yearn for how he made me feel, I knew he was just a band-aid for all the deep cuts I had received from all I had been through.

In part, he saw me the same way my abusers saw me: a sexual object, masking his thoughts with sweet words and constant connections. He made sure I'd never forget him.

I continued being food for his addiction, long after I had walked away. I asked him to stay away from my work, but to him, that translated to a reason to come daily. He would come to my place of work with his new lady, hoping to hurt me, and those visits would be followed by a sweet text about how good it was to see me.

I learned to not respond, as giving someone like him the air to breathe was toxic. Any response from me translated into the notion that he still "had me."

I eventually left that job and learned he died a few years later at the age of fifty-three from pancreatic cancer. RIP.

I'd recently seen Gianni and learned that he was diagnosed with cancer also, but he's in remission and doing better.

It was somewhat freeing to see him, talk with him, and have zero frustration, sadness, anger, or regret.

I knew that the time we spent together was meant be part of my journey.

MACK

"We'll be going the roads again, Con."

My dad would say this occasionally, but he rarely meant it. It was a phrase he used when I'd be looking for a few pounds (equivalent to a few dollars) and he'd give me what he had in his pocket. "Going the roads" meant "homeless," without food or money.

One of my fondest memories of my dad was walking to and from the neighbor's home at night. My dad and I, his hands behind his back with my fist nestled in the warmth of his palm. He would close his fingers and my hand felt safe, warm, and the perfect fit.

Sometimes, the only light we needed was from the moon. Other nights we'd need to bring the torch, and it would light up a foot or two ahead of our steps.

The walks were always along the *boreens*: unpaved, single-lane roads, with no lights, and we always managed to avoid potholes.

I loved his company and he seemed to enjoy mine also. I can easily go back there in my mind as I write about it. My dad's energy was safe.

I was not emotionally or spiritually close to my dad. He was not available for me in those departments. He was, as I like to say, "emotionally constipated." We had a special connection, nonetheless.

He was the oldest of three children. He often said there may have been one born before him, but it was never confirmed.

He was born in 1916, July 12 or July 1. His birth certificate had a different date than the one he celebrated. He believes he was born on July 1, but his birth certificate says July 12. He thinks he was christened on the twelfth. I tried to look at my own mixed dates with the same logic, but that kind of thinking wouldn't work for me, as that would mean I was christened the day before I was born.

My dad was not warm and fuzzy or affectionate. My first memory of a hug from him was when I was on the way into the Regional Hospital for a few days with a throat infection called "Quinsy". I don't remember him visiting, as he did not like the sight of blood, and I think he believed blood would be seen in hospitals.

Quinsy, a peritonsillar abscess (PTA), creates pus due to an infection behind the tonsil. Fever, throat pain, trouble opening my mouth, and a change to my voice were among the symptoms. The pain was worse on one side.

The abscess I developed was filling up very quickly and I could feel my throat closing in as I lay in the hospital bed. It was about to block my airway. Luckily, my mom was sitting next to my bed, knitting. She saw me pointing to my throat and beckoning her to get help.

The doctor didn't have time to numb the area first. He asked me to open my mouth and seconds later he lanced the abscess. The pus projected out of my mouth and onto his brown suit. The taste of it was vile, but now I could breathe. The procedure was a small price to pay to remain alive.

Another hospital stay involved getting my tonsils removed. I remember after the surgery I was very sore and people around me were throwing up from the same operation. It may have been a side effect of the anesthetic. I was able to keep my food down. The promise I made to my oldest brother, Gerry, while lying in the hospital bed, didn't last very long. I promised him I would never smoke again.

I was seventeen, and it was the first time I understood the power of cigarette addiction. It was a habit I started at twelve years old. I remember being so excited then that I learned how to inhale. The next ten years consisted of me walking around with cigarettes in one pocket and an inhaler in the other for the asthma I had developed. I rarely left home without them both.

At the time, I meant what I said to Gerry. I was done. My throat was sore, and in that moment, it was my truth as I felt nothing but pain. The addiction to the nicotine had subsided.

That freedom was short lived, though. As soon as I was without the IV drip, I found the "smoking room" in the hospital and was back into the addiction before I was discharged.

There were many nights prior when I smoked so many cigarettes at the neighbor's house that I would literally throw away the box with a few in it on my walk home at night. Again, I felt done in that moment, no more cigarettes for me. But, as soon as my eyes opened in the morning, my first thought was, "I hope it didn't rain last night so I can find the box of cigarettes I threw over the stone wall."

As soon as I got dressed, I was back up the *boreen*, looking for the spot I tossed them. Another promise I was unable to keep.

I didn't know I was an addict. I didn't use that word when I would think of a cigarette. Instead, I would think, " . . . it helps me relax." It was partly an escape, a connection I only got from smoking. It always welcomed my return. Me and the cigarette, we were good as long as I had the inhaler, which I needed daily.

Today I see the insanity of having asthma and smoking. I was talking with my nephew's boyfriend during a visit home about asthma and cigarettes. He's living that same addiction. I shared with him the insanity of having cigarettes in one pocket and my inhaler in the other and he replied, "I keep mine in the same pocket."

We both chuckled and I knew he was not ready to make any changes.

Growing up, when we would say the Rosary together on our knees, as a family every night, I remember our white cat jumping on my dad's back and nestling around his neck. He was warmer than a scarf and my dad was never bothered by him. Maybe he was saying the Rosary too. His purr echoed in the silence as he lay next to me at times.

Daddy took road trips with his friend Sonny Ford, who used to deliver sand to various places in Ireland. He would come home with a piece of cardboard, a makeshift journal, and a Biro he used to write the names of all the towns he passed along the way. It fascinated him, and he would talk about it for days and reread his notes.

One of the many stories Daddy shared with me over the years, was the morning he woke up with not a penny to his name. He asked Mammy to ask Granny for a loan, and the five pounds he got was the start of the flow of money. He was never without a pound since that day. I feel the gratitude in his story even now as I remember it. His years of letter writing to me were never without gratitude.

He had a positive outlook on life and was rarely ever down.

Another story was about Mr. Murray, who owned a hotel and land and a castle called Cregg. There was a forest behind the castle and my dad was given permission by Mr. Murray to enter that forest whenever he needed wood for the fire. Daddy could take as much as he needed whenever he needed it and he took advantage of that and was grateful for it.

In those days, my dad also sold calves when he could, to make some extra money. Mr. Murray bought one of those calves even before it was ready for market and paid a fair price that my dad agreed to.

A few months later, Daddy had an opportunity to meet Mr. Murray again. This time, Mr. Murray put an extra fifty pounds in Daddy's shirt pocket, on top of the price he originally paid for the calf. As he was putting the pounds in Daddy's pocket, Mr. Murray told him he'd gotten more meat from that calf than he expected, and he wanted my dad to make some additional profit.

My dad always referred to Mr. Murray as "a very nice man."

My dad was grateful for more than we knew or ever realized back then. More importantly, his love ran deeply, even if he never uttered the word "love" to his mom, his wife, or his kids. I once asked him, "Why didn't you tell your mother you loved her?" His reply came without hesitation: "Sure, I didn't need to tell her, she knew it."

He and his siblings were born in, and into, a thatched house, *the* thatched house that I was also raised in. More than likely, his own dad was not in the room, or even in the house, during those births.

It's only in the last twenty years that I learned of the man that fixed my ankle when I'd broken it around Christmastime one year. I was riding on my brother's shoulders when he stepped on a Lego lying on the hard, concrete floor. Down we went, my ankle breaking in the process.

The "bone setter" was the local vet, or a man that people would take their animals to if they'd broken a leg. It was said he had a gift, no medical training, and his knowledge was likely learned from an uncle or father that came before him. Some received the gift when their father passed on.

I remember coming home from the "bone setter" with a very interesting contraption on my ankle, made from wood and nails. No plaster of Paris. Acton was the bone setter's name. I was in this contraption for a few weeks until my ankle healed. Never to this day have I had an issue with it. He may have been a healer before his time.

My dad never thought he would get married. He thought his job was to be a good son. He also had, as he described, a bad chest, and asthma ran in our family. The house was a haven for it, always damp, with open, smoky turf fires.

He often shared stories about the nights as a young lad that he would go to bed at a reasonable hour and when his mother was in bed, he would get up again and sit by the fire to get what he called "comfort." He never wanted to bother his mother, so many nights he would be sitting up in front of the fire until the first light of day, as he found it harder to breathe lying down.

He would pretend he was in bed, as he never wanted to cause trouble. Little did he know the smoke from the open fire was not helping his lungs. Nevertheless, in a sitting-up position, breathing was easier.

I can relate to this as there were many nights over the years when lying down made it difficult for me to breathe. Propped-up pillows helped to ease the chest, but it made a good night's sleep impossible, and restless. I used to wish for daylight so I could get up.

Given that I shared a bed with him and Mammy, there was no hiding. I was always blessed to have the "green bottle" medicine, which would give me some relief until the inhaler was invented. My dad would often say, "Well, that's the best invention ever." He was referring to the Ventolin inhaler, still in use today. The cost is around $70 today, but we didn't have to pay back then at home.

Ned Mack, his dad, died at the age of eighty-eight. Nora, his beloved mom, died at age seventy-seven. Mack also had a sister and brother, both transitioning long before him.

An early picture of Mack

Daddy was a "ganger," a foreman of a gang of laborers. In Ireland, it's the person who superintends the work of a gang, or several workers. I don't recall him being a ganger, I only knew him to be a farmer. I saw the record books he kept when he was a ganger.

When his dad passed, it was his job to care for his mother. He loved this woman like no other. His exact words when he described her: "I will never forget, I used to go back to her room every morning and I used to ask, 'Will you be gettin' up today?' Some days she would, and sit by the fire in the armchair, some days she'd say, 'I'm more comfortable here.' Then I would bring her the tea in bed.

"The day she died, I went back to see her, and she said, 'I don't feel well, go back for Mrs. Cahill next door.' When Mrs. Cahill came to the house, my mother told us where everything was. She was a very organized lady. She died just like a child, peacefully. I never saw anyone die before, or since. Three years earlier, my father had died in bed. When we got up, he was dead. We got frightened. There was only the two of us in the house."

I loved how solid his knowing was. The Irish in that generation didn't speak their feelings. Some may still struggle. It took me going to a therapist at age twenty-three to learn what the word "love" was and how to articulate it. It was an education unto itself. My wish is that one day it will be a subject taught in a classroom, just like Irish, English, and Math. I keep hope open for that day.

Today I know communication is an art and not everyone's drawing is the same, but if we take the time to learn how the other person thinks, and how they are impacted from our art, many more colors can be added to the canvas of life.

A common phrase from my dad was, "Sure, what harm." It could be his reply to many different situations or stories he was listening to. "You may be as well off without him" was the one-liner he said to me when I shared with him, many years ago, that I had disowned the uncle that abused me. It was part of my healing journey. His one-liner felt very supportive.

He also had no hesitation if he didn't know something. "Well, I didn't know *that*," he'd say. Here are some other favorite expressions of his:

"Well, well, well . . . " He'd say this when he was bothered, almost like a sigh.

"If the ass heard that, he'd kick ye." His response to stupid questions.

"The devil a use in talking . . . " When someone wasn't listening to him.

"Ye'd be going on . . . " Not stopping, almost until something breaks.

"There's great clomper on ye" Someone doing something they shouldn't.

"Well, give it up and down to ye" A great compliment to someone.

"The devil is shook on ye."

That last expression, he'd usually use when he was frustrated or annoyed with my behavior or if I didn't come home for a day or two when I was between fifteen and seventeen. His most memorable line was, *"Don't do that to your mother again!"*

He knew I would be fine and would come back when I wanted to, but my mom's nature was a little different. My mom would say, "I'm a worry wart, I was a born worrier."

Many times, over the years I would ask Daddy, "How old are you?" and I would always get the same answer, "Ninety-two." He would say this when he was in his sixties, seventies, and eighties.

He must have been manifesting it, as he transitioned a few weeks after his ninety-second birthday.

On the day he turned ninety-two, I called my sister to have her put our dad on speaker phone. I wanted to ask him, "How old are you?" I said to my sister, "This will be the first time he will not be lying about his age. We were giddy with excitement to hear his answer. He was in good spirits that day, and fully with it, so it was the perfect time.

I heard my sister ask our dad that famous question, "Daddy, how old are you? He replied without hesitation with the number "nineteen" followed by his wonderful laugh. His next words were, "I'm ninety-two."

I do believe we become our thoughts. He lived that long because he was saying it all of those years to his subconscious. Either way, whether he manifested that or not, it was his time to transition.

I made my own rules. I went to bed whenever I felt like it, no boundaries. There was no guidance. My dad was more like a friend. I loved to hang out with him, like a buddy, not a parent. He was only available physically, not emotionally. He was not able to communicate, or he chose not to communicate, as he never was used to that way of life.

He never expressed feelings. His age may have had something to do with that. He was in his fifties when I was born, and I wouldn't have traded him for anything in the world. He expressed himself beautifully through his writings. Each letter I wrote him, I asked about twenty or thirty questions.

We had no phone in our home when I left it, and it was five years later when they finally got one installed. When I called home, I would call the neighbors and ask them to get Mammy, and I'd tell them I'd call back in an hour.

The call was always sad for my mom and she cried through most of it. Her baby was gone to America. My perception was that I was free and having fun. It saddened me to hear her so sad.

When I left home, my dad would barely look at an airplane flying by, as he never understood how it stayed up in the sky. Not to mention he'd never get in one to come visit.

It was five years after I left Ireland, that my dad's love for my brother and me became louder than his fears of flying.

My mom shared the story that as he sat in his seat on the plane, he turned to my mom and said, "When are we going to get in the plane?" He was expecting to have to walk out to the tarmac and walk up the stairs like the private or smaller aircraft, like he had seen on TV, maybe.

Many things fascinated him about America, from my ability to drive the roads here—on the wrong side—to walking around Home Depot or Lowe's. One of the places I showed him was a pet cemetery, but I don't think he ever fully took that story in. Animals in Ireland back then would never be treated to burials. They weren't even treated that well when they were alive, not to mention when they died, so his mind was unable to wrap it around pets having their resting place, like humans.

I was not aware that he would be taking that trip with my mom, her second trip to America.

My mom and dad were staying with my mom's sister, and my brother had picked them up at the airport. I thought only my mom was coming to visit. When I saw my dad for the first time in five years, I was literally speechless. Anyone who knows me today, knows I am far from speechless.

He looked frail, old, and shorter. I sat on his lap or sat next to him the entire evening. It was one of the most beautiful moments I have experienced in my lifetime.

I bought slippers for Mammy and a bouquet of flowers. My dad was my gift. We talked for the entire evening. We laughed a lot.

Our next visit included a long walk near my aunt's house where my parents stayed, a view of Boston's city skyline in the distance. I was living in a studio apartment at the time, so I didn't have a guest room for them.

I smile as I remember taking them out to dinner. Daddy would always want all of his food on one plate, not side plates. He would always wonder, "Why do they have to dirty all of them plates?" I made sure that the vegetables on the side plate, made it to his main plate so that he could enjoy his dinner.

He would peel the skins off his baked potato and shake his head at the sight of me eating the skins, thinking, "Are you that poor and hungry that you have to eat the skins?"

Within a few weeks, we were back at Logan Airport, saying our goodbyes. I did not know when I'd see them again, as I had not heard back from the Green Card applications I had submitted.

For three years in a row, I'd applied for different types of lottery visas. In the third year, I received a letter from the Irish Embassy in Dublin to appear at 8 a.m. for an interview to get a Green Card. At the time, I had two and a half years of sobriety under my belt.

It had been seven years since I'd last set foot on Irish soil.

A trip home would awaken all the memories.

MAMMY

I've heard that mother-daughter, or father-son, relationships are the most important because the parents more readily imprint on their children how to become women and men.

It took many years for me to experience that connection with my mom.

She was born in 1933 and was one of twins. Her parents had no idea they were having twins, but the second child was found in what they thought was the afterbirth. There was movement, and it was the other baby.

Paddy, my mom's twin brother, dies at the age of thirty-four from a form of cancer, leukemia, we believe. He was being treated in Dublin Hospital for some time, but it was rarely talked about.

There were no incubators back in those days, and the story goes that people were born at home, usually with a neighbor who may have had experience with being present for another neighbor's delivery. That would have been the extent of their training. Today, we'd know them as midwives or doulas.

The trust was there, even if the training wasn't, and the mom knew she wouldn't be alone. The men in those days usually left the house during the birthing and returned to find a child (or children). It's unclear how premature they were, but we know both twins together weighted around three pounds.

It's amazing that they survived as well as they did. Granny had to love, nurture, and care for them along with their older sister, who was only eleven months old. Three more children followed later. The twins were so small they got baths in a mixing bowl. Granny also rubbed goose lard on their skin daily and kept them next to the fire to keep them warm and alive.

My mom's journey started in 1933 and ended in 2016. Her life was filled with grandkids, visits to and from the neighbors, and countless cups of tea, but also worry, anxiety, Holy water, blessed candles, countless Rosaries, and beautiful Irish-knit Aran sweaters that she made, as well as cardigans, socks, and caps that she also made herself.

The Rosary beads, Holy water, and blessed candles emerged during storms,

surgeries, and times of illness.

Many times, I would call her and ask her to light a candle for someone here in the U.S. who was going through a difficult time, and I knew it would be done. My brother Gerry carries on that tradition to this day.

Each time she would light a candle for someone here in the U.S., or for a neighbor in her village, she never failed to take credit once they got through the surgery or when the sick got well. "My prayers were answered," she'd say. I loved the faith she had in prayers.

One of the many stories she told over the years was about the woman with long, white hair, known as the "Banshee." The Banshee were among the oldest faerie folk of Ireland, associated as strongly as shamrocks. Stories about them appearing the night before another soul transitioned were plentiful.

Mammy described them to a tee and never changed her story, even during the last few months of her life, when she would reminisce about her childhood.

She saw the Banshee sitting on stone steps that led up to a field. The Banshee had a very distinct cry, and it was heard the night before a sick neighbor passed away.

My mom also worked in a haunted castle, Medieval Tulira Castle, in the village

of Ardrahan in County Galway, Ireland. She often talked about "the great hall" and how she washed the floors on her knees. My mom was grateful for the job and to be able to make some money.

She would often tell the story of hearing noises coming from upstairs and dishes breaking in the kitchen, but no one was there when she would check. It didn't scare her enough to quit. The ghosts and spirits must have been friendly. I enjoyed hearing about them, but I'm fine with not experiencing them directly myself.

The castle is privately owned nowadays, by a Dutch couple. They have restored it to its original look. I was trying to find it and take a tour the last time I was home, but I was not able to get past the gate. My mom got paid a half-crown once a month there, equivalent to about thirty U.S. cents back then.

The Sunday dinner was always boiling when we returned from Mass. The bacon would be on the second or third boil to get rid of the salt, and the cabbage would be added in the third boil.

It was creamed by the time it reached our lips. Carrots were often included and of course spuds, with their jackets on, would be boiling in another saucepan. They were always on the side. Salt and butter were always on the table despite the salty bacon.

Mammy had her own expressions, although quite different than Daddy's:

"If I burned the house, I couldn't find it" Looking for something, to no avail.

"I searched high up and low down" Same as above. (She searched a lot).

"It's in the hot press or the rubbish drawer" When all else fails, it's there.

"Ye oughta' say the Rosary" A daily expression.

"Your bladder is very near your eyes" When we cried about something.

"It won't melt ye"' Being sent to the shop, complaining that it was raining.

Feathers were floating into her home many times over the last few years of her life, but we had no chickens to blame. In the "spirit world," feathers are messages from angels. She let us know each time another one would come in through her open door or window.

My mom was constantly putting herself down; her self-esteem was low. She had little education and that left her feeling something less than she was. She'd say things like, "Sure, I'm stupid." Knowing what low self-esteem felt like, I always tried to help her think differently.

Years earlier, during one of my therapy sessions with Dr. Fanger, he'd given me a line that changed my thinking, and I'd repeat it to my mom during each visit with her. I would say, "Mammy, you are not stupid, you were simply uninformed about many life lessons and didn't get the additional help that nowadays is available."

I'm not sure she was able to digest this information, but I would share it with her anyway. Her intake of information was limited and how she would repeat it later was often questionable, as the details were usually incomplete.

Growing up, my mom was emotionally and spiritually absent in our relationship. She was always there physically though, as her primary job was being a wife and a mother. "Mother" here does not mean "nurturing."

Today, I wonder how much the loss of her first daughter might have played a part in her absence. It's impossible to give what you don't have.

I didn't realize just how absent she was until I was around twenty-five. I can still see one our neighbor's moms kissing their children goodbye as they ran out the door to play. When I'd see that affection with their kids, it seemed strange, foreign, like they were the weirdos.

I never, ever received kisses and hugs from my parents. Their brand of love for their children was what I would call "operational" or "functional," and that derived from their complete lack of education and understanding about parenting beyond whatever they learned from their own uneducated, impoverished parents.

So it's no wonder to me now that the only understanding of love and affection I had back then came from inappropriate touching and abuse.

My mom was a great one for visiting the neighbors as often as she could, going to anniversary Masses, or to engage cups of tea, and she always went home to her "home" house, home to Granny, to the house she grew up in. Home to the same home where my uncle abused me for years. The house that was my own private "war zone." What Mammy called "home" became my nightmare.

For all the recollections and early laments about the relationship with my mom, all the differences between us were erased six months before she passed.

I learned then that she was a beautiful soul.

Mammy

FORGIVENESS

Every self-help book I ever read always ended with "forgiveness" as the last chapter, and I would always skip it.

I was not even ready to read about it, let alone allow that ridiculous idea into my head.

At that time, forgiveness had a very different meaning to me. Somehow, I thought forgiveness meant accepting that what happened to me was OK. I now know what the word really means: pardon, absolution, exoneration, remission, dispensation, indulgence, clemency, and especially *mercy*.

I held on to the notion that the power was in my "non-forgiveness" and was somehow locked up in resentment. It would be much later in my journey that I learned or experienced otherwise. The power would also become prayer for me, again to be applied when I was ready.

One of my experiences in forgiveness was during a trip home to Ireland. In a hotel bar, I recognized a man who had abused me. He didn't recognize me. I had grown up, I had a black pantsuit on, with high heels. I was feeling very adult and, to some degree, powerful and confident about who I was. Maybe I could even add sexy to that description. The sexy feeling came from the confidence I felt, not from exposing my legs or cleavage.

He was with a mutual friend of ours who smiled at me from across the room. I was there with my sister, sitting at the bar, when our friend approached us and offered to pay for our drinks. He was a gentleman, and my sister loved all the free drinks.

I had sparkling water. She was drinking something a little stronger. To be Irish and not drinking alcohol in a pub is not a common thing. "I just don't drink," is what I said when I was asked. Other times I would say, "I'm driving," or I could have said, "I've been sober five years now." That would have been a conversation stopper for sure.

When our friend rejoined us, his friend, the one he'd been sitting with, and who was one of my abusers, said he wanted to buy us the next drink. He was shocked it was me, all grown up, and he asked how old I was when I babysat for him. I reminded him I was fifteen to sixteen then. He had no response to that. He asked what I was doing in the U.S.

I'm sure I told him about my job, but I also remember telling him I was writing a book. He immediately said, "I hope I'm not in it." In the moment, that translated to me as, "I'm sorry, what I did was wrong."

I never heard these words from him directly, but his fear of being in the book was enough.

This was the closest I have come to receiving an apology. From anyone. Ever.

It took me thirty years to fully forgive my primary abuser, my uncle. I had forgiven him in the sense he no longer owned or affected my emotions. I was able to be in the same room with him, but I used much of my energy refraining from talking to him, thinking that was what I was supposed to do.

If I talked to him, I thought he would interpret that as meaning everything was OK, like he'd never done anything wrong. More than likely, he wasn't thinking about what he did, as he never fully owned it. Instead, he more likely viewed his behavior as "messing with me" and so long as he didn't enter me, my mom was OK with it.

° ° °

Byron Katie is a speaker, author, and spiritual innovator who teaches a method of self-inquiry known as "The Work." It is a process born directly out of her own experiences with severe depression.

She is one of the many people I have learned from over the years. She teaches people to examine their own thoughts and helps us—helped me—see that it was my thoughts that were making me feel what I was feeling and not the actual situation. She had a profound impact on me, and I carry that with me daily and try to teach others.

When I learned how to apply her four inquiry questions, I was able to regain power over my own mind. Those questions are:

Q1. Is it true?

Q2. Can you absolutely know that it's true?

Q3. How do you react, what happens, when you believe that thought?

Q4. Who would you be without that thought?

AA taught me: "When we are disturbed by people, places, or things, it's inside we need to look, not outside."

I liked the power in owning my responses, which led to "my" attitude, no matter who I was angry at, or what was done to me. It was how I responded that determined my attitude.

We all have triggers. Some are good and they are easy to manage and enjoy, but it's the less pleasant ones that can leave us in turmoil when we have not mastered our own mind and thoughts.

One of the lines my good pal Gregg would say to me over, and over, and over again in my early sobriety, when I felt like I was going crazy, was, "Stop thinking."

I thought it was the most insane suggestion to give someone, especially me. Many times, I would hang up on him, but he was always so calm and seemed to have his act together.

Our mind limits us. It can keep us in a box. You tell someone your age and you are automatically put in a category of the "should." Typically, someone my age *should* be married with kids, or someone who is nineteen *should* be in college, or if you practice a certain religion, that's another box to be put in. Catholic, Jewish, Protestant, and other religions all come with fixed assumptions.

I could never be boxed in. I liked to color between and outside the lines.

I have a fond memory of being in Ireland, visiting home, and in a conversation with an Irish lad, I mentioned, "I was always the black sheep of the family." His reply made me laugh. He said, "No. You were the white one."

That gave me a different level of thinking. While I digested it, we both laughed. I've held on to that, as it feels better than feeling like I was the odd one out.

Maybe I was the only one who was *not* odd. I'm sure my family would disagree, but they are not the ones writing this book, so they will have to share their thoughts elsewhere.

Forgiving others is essential for spiritual growth. I felt I had forgiven my uncle, but I also made sure I would not be in his company for long, if ever. If I could avoid it altogether, I would—and I did for years, except for two occasions: when he was traveling back to Ireland from Boston with my mom, and in a moment beside my mom's hospice bed.

I was in my forties and taking my mom to the airport to meet my uncle. Once there, I got her settled into her wheelchair so she could get through the airport more comfortably. I had her passport and I needed to meet my uncle to give it to him. We sat at the same table for a short period of time, exchanging five or six sentences, if that. I remained distant. I was only there for my mom.

After I said goodbye, my eyes filled with tears, not because of the goodbye, but because the little kid in me wanted to hear "I'm sorry" from him. That was not going to happen. I was alone again as I walked back to my car after saying goodbye to my mom and that man who abused me for many years.

I felt good that I was able to be there for my mom and not have to dissociate or leave my body.

The day I truly felt forgiveness will be etched in my heart, mind, and soul, for all the years to come. I believe there are many levels of forgiveness, but this last piece was the final layer. I was not expecting it, but I felt it at all levels.

It was a mild December morning, eight or nine years after seeing my mom and her brother in the same room. As always, I'd gotten to the hospital before 8 a.m. to get an update on my mom from her caretaker.

She told me that my mom had a good night's sleep, so she was full of life that morning, singing, sharing stories, and pain free. I videoed her singing some of her favorite tunes that morning.

After her breakfast, she drifted off into a deep sleep, mouth open, on her back, so her breaths became deep with a rattle to them. This was something I was used to from my home care experiences.

One of her frequent visitors was her brother—my uncle, the one who abused me. I typically would leave the room and get a cup of tea at the cafeteria so as not to be in his energy and to give them privacy.

This time was different. Something had shifted; it felt like a miracle in part.

My mom looked like she could take her last breath at any minute, Her breaths were deep and she was unresponsive when her name was called. My uncle looked scared, worried, and I saw compassion in his face and eyes for the first time ever. It may also have been the first time I looked him in the eyes.

I saw him as a scared human being and not as my abuser.

Instead of leaving that morning, I pulled up a chair so he could sit next to her and I shared with him the playful videos I had taken of her earlier that morning. His fears lifted.

I felt compassion for him, and that shift inside me made being in this man's company no longer uncomfortable from any aspect of my being.

Was that a miracle? I'm saying, "Yes!"

PARTING IS A GIFT

The silence after his last breath was deafening.

I was not alone. The hospice nurse and the patient's wife were also in the room as he transitioned.

When I took off his oxygen mask, his wife screamed at me, in a different language. I don't know what she said, but she didn't want to see her lifelong partner leaving this life. They had been together seventy or more years.

They were both Holocaust survivors.

He was in his nineties and I was part of his care for the last two weeks of his life. His daughter was a doctor, but she had a difficult time seeing him from the day he was put on oxygen around the clock. It was her dad, not just a patient.

She had moved him from New York to her home in Newton, MA, where she provided care for him during the day.

The room always had soft music playing in the background. He enjoyed symphony music. He was no longer eating. We were just keeping him comfortable, safe, and clean.

His skin drank the moisturizer I gave it daily and his lips were always layered with Vaseline. Lemon swabs kept his mouth moist as he was not awake to swallow. He seemed to experience flashbacks at different times and his loud moans and cries didn't come from current pain. The morphine and Ativan were taking care of that.

It was the day his daughter left to pick up her own daughter from school. She always left at 3 p.m., but this day she left at 2 thinking it was 3. I called her to come home ten minutes after she left, as her father was taking his last breath. He passed peacefully.

Each patient I got to be with as they parted, felt like a gift. I was a stranger to the family a week or ten days earlier, but within a very short time I would become a source of comfort and continuity for the patients. I was able to bring my prior experience with other cases, which seemed to ease some of the family's questions.

No amount of information can ease the pain of loss. Nothing really prepares someone for death.

A wonderful soul used to call me "Irish." He was still very conscious when we met. He had adult children who hovered around him as much as they possibly could, and he tried to get some sleep at night. One daughter had a very difficult time letting him go and questioned me every morning about what our night was like.

Some nights, he was quiet and seemed to be at peace. Other nights he would want to chat. He spoke so fondly of his kids and shared wonderful stories about when they were young. He remembered standing outside their bedroom doors at night saying a prayer. He wanted to make sure God was watching over them while they were sleeping.

He too passed comfortably. I said goodbye to him on a Saturday morning as it seemed he might be slipping away, but I was back for my 11 p.m. shift Monday night. He was still alive and wanted to make sure I was there to support his family. He took his last breath ten minutes after I walked through the door.

As always, I stayed with the patient until the body was removed from the home. We always suggested that the family stay in a different room and not watch this process. Their loved one is removed in a black bag, a memory that no one wants etched in their mind.

James was one of my favorite souls. I managed care for him for five years. He received 24/7 care, and his son would come from New York on weekends.

I took him to his doctor and learned he had a mass and it looked like cancer, but they were not able to get a good look with the scope test they did. It was decided that additional testing would be too invasive. The doctor reassured us that he would be dead long before the cancer would catch up to him. James was in his nineties, and some cancers grow more slowly in an aged body.

We were completely relieved taking him home that day and it was never talked about again. We trusted the doctor.

I was on vacation in Iceland with my friend Bob when I would receive daily up-dates on James. On the Thursday of that week, his caregiver said his tummy was a little swollen, but he wasn't complaining. His appetite was normal, but she was concerned. I returned from my trip that Sunday and was in his home that afternoon. He had a big smile as always when he saw me walk through the door. It was greeted with a smile from me.

His tummy didn't look good. It was quite distended and according to his son, he had no appetite that morning.

It was time to call his general practitioner; I knew this was not good. From the description I gave to his doctor, he said, "We have two choices. One: start hospice now at home, or two: take him to the hospital."

James didn't understand why he needed to go to the hospital. I knew his son would need more information before he'd agree to start hospice at home.

I packed a bag for him to stay a few days in the hospital after I called the ambulance. James didn't really understand what was happening, but he trusted me and my judgment.

We learned later that evening that his mass had doubled in size in two months. It was inoperable. James was sent home Friday to start hospice.

The next couple of days I was by his side. I cancelled my massage clients on Saturday as I didn't want to leave him. We didn't get much sleep, as he was restless, and I was on the couch in the same room. In the middle of the night, he would call my name. "I'm here," I said. He didn't need anything most times. He just needed to know I was there, that he was not alone.

Hours before his passing, he was urinating blood, which I didn't want him to see. That would have scared him.

He was a strong man and well known in his community. He had a career as a neuropsychologist, teaching part time at Harvard. We had the priest come around 10 p.m. because we knew James's time was limited. He transitioned at 11 p.m. while the priest prayed over him.

His body was removed a couple of hours after being placed in the black bag. That part never gets easier. I wish there were a more pleasant way of removing a body, but I'm sure the body doesn't care at that point.

There were several souls that passed on my shifts. Some peacefully. With others, their breath gets quite labored.

My dad's passing was, to this day, the most peaceful I have ever witnessed.

Three deep breaths and he was gone.

The sound of his soul, leaving his body was a whisper.

THE LONG WARD

"It is so much darker when a light goes out than it would have been if it had never shone." - John Steinbeck

Mack was admitted to the Regional Hospital, Galway due to severe COPD and colitis. He was ninety years young then.

When he left the hospital, he needed more care than my mom could give him, so he was transferred to an old monastery that served as a nursing home, Corrandulla Nursing Home.

I was home for his ninetieth birthday, when he was still a resident at the nursing home. He was there twenty-three days in total until he suffered what appeared to be a stroke. He wound up going back to the hospital.

When he was discharged, he was transferred to much nicer accommodations, as my sister made room for him in her home. The support from her husband was inexorable and his reply to the reality that a hospital bed may not fit through their front door was, "Sure, we can take out a window." He was all in, 100 percent.

It made the most sense to stay with my sister, as she had already been by his side daily at the nursing home. She had spoken with her husband and three sons, and they were all on board. The youngest was not very impressed—until he got to play with the hospital bed and the Hoya Lift.

One of the many sweet stories that my sister shared with me over the next two years was about her youngest son. He was curious and was enjoying the "toys" that came with Mack. He asked, "When Mack dies, can we keep his electric bed?" It still makes me smile as I think of his innocence today. He was six years old at the time.

They set Daddy up with the nicest room in the house, a warm fireplace, and a flatscreen TV with a remote control. He never did appreciate remote controls, but there was always some young lad around to operate it for him.

My sister's husband had a great rapport with my dad, and he would make the fire daily before Mack was taken out of bed. Daddy had two different ladies, home health aides, that he bonded very nicely with, especially Mary. God love her and all she did for him.

He would be watching the clock knowing the time she would show up. They had a ritual. When she would leave, she'd look in the window and they'd give one another the thumbs-up sign followed by a smile. Mary is now in Heaven also, she died way too young, in her early fifties. I believe it was from an infection that went untreated. RIP.

° ° °

Methicillin-Resistant Staphylococcus Aureus: MRSA.

It meant Daddy was admitted yet again to the Regional Hospital, Galway. It also meant he could have a private room.

We were not grateful for the MRSA infection, but we were for the privacy. In addition to the MRSA, he had bone degeneration in his back, and he was unable to walk. He was in excruciating pain most of the time. Nurses would check on him often as I sat by his side. He knew he was not alone.

Our family members came and went, but I wanted to spend every hour possible with him as I knew it was a matter of days before he would pass away.

He wanted to die at home, but he was also very easygoing and knew we did what we needed to keep him comfortable and hydrated and pain free, and this could only occur in a hospital setting. Arranging an in-home hospice in Ireland is a slower process than in America, and we didn't know how much time we had.

He had developed an infection that made him delirious at times, and it masked the agonizing pain in his lower back. When the antibiotics reached the infection, the pain would return.

The first time I heard him roar from the pain was while I was in the U.S. on the phone with my sister. I can still remember hearing it. I asked her if he was reaching for something and I knew any movement that involved his lower back would cause the unbearable pain. The oral meds that my sister gave him made him sleep more, mitigating the pain but simultaneously causing dehydration.

My dad was never a complainer and only used to get a headache periodically. He would take some Tylenol and tie one of Mammy's nylons around his head to change the pressure and relieve his pain. Lying down also helped.

There was no reaching the pain now in his lower back. He was in a fetal position in his hospital bed one evening, after Dr. Bell got his infection under control, and she suggested my dad be transferred yet again to a nursing home.

I knew he would be back in the same spin cycle again. The pain meds made him sleep a lot and they dehydrated him. He was unable to take in fluids. He had been through enough.

Pain is necessary but suffering is optional, and I knew his wishes.

He said to me on one of the twenty-one days I was with him, "I don't care what you do to me, Connie, but get me out of this pain." A few years earlier we had talked about what to do when the time comes, and his words were very clear. His exact words were, "Let me go to God."

Working with hospice in the U.S., I assisted with keeping many patients comfortable during their last journey. Pain is pain, regardless of whether it's cancer or degeneration of bone. Keeping my dad comfortable and pain-free was my goal, and my mission.

I requested a meeting with the palliative care team to assess my dad, and they were able to talk to him directly and get his permission to take over his case. This started a process of administering various medicine cocktails to help relieve the pain that wasn't going to be leaving on its own anytime soon.

"Are you in pain, Patrick?" they asked. "Well, I am, Doctor," he would say. Their next question was, "Will we give you medicine to make it better?" "DO!" was his reply.

We used to joke with him often, to have him say please or thank you when it was appropriate. In his day-to-day life with the family, "please" and "thank you" were not always words he would use in his sentences. When he would ask for something, we used to joke when he would say, "No." We would say, "No what?" like you would when teaching a child about manners. His humorous side would always emerge, and he would say, "No way."

The day he agreed to be treated for his pain, I knew was a bittersweet day for all of us. He was put on a morphine pump with 10cc given over a twenty-four-hour period, and that was increased daily. A top-up was also allowed should he have breakthrough pain. I was his voice as he wouldn't, and couldn't, ask for it. I didn't want him to wait until he was in pain. He was kept comfortable, and that was my focus each time I would think his days were coming to an end. He passed away eleven days into the cocktail.

Eleven days before he took his last breath, his MRSA cleared up and he was going to be taken out of quarantine in his private room and put in what was called the "Long Ward." This ward was for acute patients where they were constantly monitored.

I remember it like it was yesterday. I was with him when he was transferred to the Long Ward. It was a Saturday night. I leaned up against the double doors of the Long Ward and thought, "What a horrible place to die," with tears pouring down my face, but knowing it was also the best place for him.

Looking back now, a place like the Galway Hospice would have been the more peaceful place and with excellent care. I was not aware of its existence at that time, however. I knew the only thing I would change at that time was my own thinking, as his situation was not going to improve, but his pain would.

Within twenty-four hours, the horrible place started to feel like home to me and I got to know most of the other fifteen patients in the ward. He was on the left-hand side without a view. A few more old lads like himself were also there. He was cared for, given a sponge bath daily. He was comfortable, safe, warm, and loved in a way I didn't know I was even capable of. He was the quietest man in the room and looked the most comfortable also. I knew he needed acute care, which was why he was placed there, and two nurses covered that ward.

I decided to stay with him for the last eleven days of his life. I borrowed another patient's recliner at night to get some sleep, whereas he used it during the day. It was pale blue in color and the material was vinyl. I borrowed two hospital pillows to create a comfortable bed. I felt useful, even if just to hold my dad's hand so he knew he was not alone.

It was a busy place, too. A drunk was admitted one night and he was so loud and intoxicated he had no idea where he was or why he was there. He was placed next to my dad. He slept most of the next day and was as quiet as a lamb when he woke up. He must have eventually changed his thinking to "Being in this bed is better than being on a sidewalk, drunk."

The lovely man across from my dad needed a caregiver each night. His over-head light was always on, and he didn't sleep much. He was not a happy camper. He had a morphine pump in his pocket as he walked around with the caregiver. He had Parkinson's that went untreated for a long time and his body was not responding to his mind. He was angry a good deal of the time, but always asked, "How is your dad?" when he was able to talk.

The man on the other side was a priest, ninety-four years young. The youngest man was fifty-three and each day he would say, "I may be going home tomorrow." He was lying on a sand bed set to 105 degrees, trying to heal his wounds. His legs had been amputated from below the knees and he was paralyzed, so by the time he was aware he had an infection, it had broken through his skin and spread throughout his body.

Each time the lights would go off, he would do his upper body exercises to try to maintain some muscle conditioning. He was a sweet soul and he asked me every morning as I walked by, "How's your dad today?" and I was always able to say, "He's comfortable."

I'm sure he was thinking he wished he could say the same. This was in August 2006, and each day he would say, "Maybe they will let me go home tomorrow." I asked one of the kind nurses one day, "Will he be going home soon? He keeps saying he might be." Her answer shocked me. She told me he'd been there since December 2005.

He validated how powerful the mind is despite the condition of the body.

o o o

Sunday morning, August 10, 2006, 9:25 a.m.

The priest was often by my dad's side during his previous stays in hospital. It was better than a pill for him. My dad had the utmost respect and faith in the Catholic priests.

My dad transitioned just before the priest had ended his Sunday morning mass. This brought me comfort as I wouldn't be surprised if Daddy had attended that Mass in his mind, even while his body rested in the hospital bed.

Each morning, as my eyes opened next to him in a chair, I always placed my hand on his tummy first to make sure he was still breathing. I had much experience with someone passing in my company but had not ever found a person dead. There was something unappealing to me about that.

Each morning, I felt the warmth of his body that still had life in it. Five nurses cleaned his body that morning as he was so frail that any sudden torque would have ended his life. They were extra gentle with him this morning.

One of the nurses came to get me, after I had stepped out for a few minutes, to tell me he was all set and that I could sit with him again.

Soon after she'd gotten me, another nurse was walking by as he was taking his last breath and I called to her. "I think he's leaving us," I said.

She quickly pulled a picture of the Sacred Heart out of her pocket and placed it on his chest and started to say the Our Father prayer. I joined her as tears poured down my cheeks.

Daddy would have been very happy to know that prayers were said over him.

I sat on the bed looking at him. His blue T-shirt matched his blue eyes. I held his hand and as I did, the volume of his breath got a little louder. It deepened, three in a row, and at his last breath, his eyes opened involuntarily. I reached out and closed them. They were as blue as the ocean. And then, silence.

It was so quiet that morning, despite the fifteen other patients around him.

You could hear a pin drop.

Daddy was gone.

The nurse let me use her cell phone to call my sister and brother. They would have to tell Mammy the news in person.

The nurse later told me she was in Galway city the day prior and went into the Abbey Church and took the Sacred Heart picture with her when she left.

The curtains were closed around him to provide privacy for the hours ahead, for family members that would come to say their goodbyes and to support one another at this time of loss.

Despite that most of Daddy's friends were predeceased, there were over four hundred names signed in the book of condolences, by people who came to pay their respects.

During one of my visits home, my dad had developed laryngitis and was unable to speak. He was still living with my sister, Noreen. I bought him a whistle and a bell, so he could call for help when he needed it.

The bell was by his side while the whistle hung on the rail of the bed, within reach. I quietly hoped he wouldn't be using these items at 2 in the morning when the family was trying to sleep, while I was back in America sleeping soundly.

My sister made sure the whistle was placed in the coffin next to him, in case he needed anything.

○ ○ ○

Daddy was laid out in a dark suit and a Gucci tie.

I often smile as I think that if he knew the cost of the tie, he'd roll over in his grave. But then, just like he didn't believe pet cemeteries existed, I'm sure he'd never have comprehended the cost of that tie.

I wanted him to go "in style."

The deep sadness I felt at the loss of my dad, was met by an even deeper connection to him somehow, one that wasn't there when he was still living. With his last breath, I felt like our souls were joined and that although his death closed a long, familiar chapter between us, another one was about to be written.

When I returned to America, I was alone, but I took him with me in my heart. I remember feeling closer to him than I did when we he was still on earth and only 3,000 miles apart.

This feeling was validated one year later, when I went home for his one-year anniversary Mass. After the plane landed in Shannon Airport, I drove to my dad's resting place, the Old Annaghdown Cemetery. Annaghdown is a stretch of stone ruins, buildings from a bygone abbey over 1,000 years old, a place somehow fitting for my dad.

I climbed over the stone wall and walked across the grassy lawn through an opening in one of the ruin walls. I turned my head to the right and saw where he was buried. His marker was there, of course, and the memory of his funeral, but I knew my dad wasn't truly there.

He was in my heart, and I carry him there always.

Daddy and me.

HARASSMENT ORDER

OkCupid was the online dating website that I was searching through when I saw a face that caught my eye. His written profile was also appealing.

Eight months later, my local Needham Police and a Dedham judge were involved with sending the man a message.

He seemed normal, but intense, nervous, and over forty-five minutes late to our first date. It was a lovely summer's evening. I sat outside a restaurant at Legacy Place in Dedham, MA. He eventually showed up, but I don't remember his excuse and I didn't remember I had also met him four years earlier for a drink, something he reminded me about a few weeks into dating.

After he reminded me of our first date years ago, I remembered he was nervous then too. He drank three or four beers during our time together then, walking me to my car after, and we never met again.

Being over twenty years sober then, I was not going to invest any time in someone who needed to consume that many beers in a short period of time, regardless of anxiety.

This time, we started dating after our OkCupid connection. The tensions got louder and when I saw him once a week, his question, "When will I see you again?" would come up moments after we sat down to eat. I was trying to enjoy the restaurant and the company. I kept thinking he'd relax soon. One of the many questions I asked him was whether he was in a relationship or dating anyone else and he always said, "No."

I got the first Hallmark card from him way too soon, in my opinion. Three weeks after meeting him, I was also given a key to his house, attached to another Hallmark card.

On the fifth or sixth date I did a "check-in" from the restaurant we ate at, on Facebook, and tagged his name. To my surprise, I received a private message from his girlfriend saying, "He has a girlfriend, you know." She also private messaged me that she was in the process of moving in with him and enrolling her son in his town to continue school, and of course he had his own story when I asked him about her. This was the beginning of me walking away.

He knew how much I loved photography, and he used to enjoy it also. I was and remain a very direct person and I said without sugar coating it, "Do not buy a camera with the intent that you and I will be spending more time together."

I also told him, "If I get one more Hallmark card, I will rip it up." It was way too much mush, love, and intense feelings, in a few short weeks. It felt uncomfortable and unsafe.

He started seeing a therapist, as I had suggested he needed help with his intense energy. I knew it was not me that was causing it. Having years of therapy under my own belt with an excellent therapist, I knew the process and how beneficial it can be, when and if one is ready to get real and become honest.

After his second, maybe third, therapy session, I met him for dinner. He was excited to tell me what he learned in therapy that day. I was happy to hear what I assumed might be an epiphany or some form of insight about himself, which is what therapy is all about.

Instead, I didn't know whether to laugh or feel sorry for him, when he shared his good news with me. He said, "My therapist and I figured it out today in session." I waited with open ears for the next line out of his mouth. "My therapist and I believe you don't know how to be loved." I later put two and two together: he was a Born Again Christian, and it was his job to show me love, his job to take me to Jesus Christ. Phew!

I quickly responded that if I were him, I would not waste my time or money talking about me in his therapy sessions, unless I was next to him, which I knew would never happen.

At this time, I had never had an encounter, as far as I know, with a Born Again Christian. I knew and loved Christians. I consider myself Christian today. I grew up Catholic and I know I love and trust the God of my understanding.

There was something telling me ending this would not be easy. I once joined him in his church. Now, a Mass in Ireland is thirty minutes long and in the U.S. it's about an hour, so I asked him how long this service was. He said around forty-five minutes.

That was about all I could handle, unless it was interesting.

He failed to mention we would get there thirty minutes before it started, and that the forty-five minutes was, in reality, more than sixty minutes, with hanging around, chatting, and mingling. After it was over, two and a half hours had passed. I was beyond my limit by the time we left, and I knew it was the first and last time I'd be joining him there.

He was beaming as he waited to introduce me to the pastor, who seemed like a nice guy even though I have never held priests of any religion on a pedestal. I respect them, yes, but I don't share my parents' belief that priests are any closer to God than I am.

I received some lectures over the next few weeks about how I should not listen to Dr. Wayne Dyer, as he taught self-reliance and was not Christian. That was the icing on the cake for me. Being told what I should do and not do, does not fly with me, especially given that Wayne Dyer was someone I called my "sponsor" for years. (Most people had an AA sponsor, but I trusted Wayne's teachings and Mark Fanger. That was all I needed.)

I received a few emails from him after I attempted to end seeing him. I believe now that he was 100 percent convinced that he was "born again" to save me, to love me, to provide for me, to care for me, and whatever other belief he had written on his script. *His* script, not mine. That read as controlling to me.

As far as I was concerned, it was over two or three months into our once-a-week get togethers. The texting back and forth from me was direct and polite. I was done, and I was clear about that. He didn't like what he was hearing and asked why I was doing this to him. He said he felt like a child who had been waiting for Santa, to receive the gift he'd always wanted, but then he broke the gift and was being punished.

I was thinking, "Yeah, 'gave us a shot and it didn't work out." Then he wanted to just be a client of mine and was willing to pay for a massage—or take me to dinner. He thought I was skilled at my massage practice and that I was able to make his neck and shoulder pain feel better.

He was right about that, as I have been able to help him, and many others, feel better with treatment. He was missing the headlines or didn't want to read: "It's Over."

There are two guys I dated in the past who remain good friends today. It's not always necessary to cut off all communication, but I knew this was different. This needed to be sealed tightly, as he was not going to give up.

Weeks had passed without contact, and I felt freedom. I never missed a single thing about him. I got a couple more private messages from the lady who called herself his girlfriend. They read something like, "We have been together for two and a half years. He tried to end it after he met you, can you please tell me how you met him, girl-to-girl? I would like to know more."

I ignored it, and then a few weeks later, I got another message from her that said, "NOTHING? You don't even respond to me?" This message didn't have a sweet tone. Her third message was the last and I responded with the same style: no reply. What they were going through was between them alone. I quietly thought, "I hope they can reconnect and live happily ever after and both of them leave me alone."

I was on a hospice case in December of that same year, doing twelve-hour shifts, mostly nights. I got a call from my good pal Leo. He and his wife had met this same man once during the few weeks we were dating. Leo's message was in part, "Hey kiddo [as he called me], you may be getting a visitor, he was here today, and he was acting very strange."

Leo was surprised to see him at his door, but invited him inside nevertheless. He started off with small talk, then asked Leo about me, not caring about the advice Leo gave him, which was, "What I know about Connie is that when she says it's over, it's over."

He proceeded to show Leo photos we had taken once, with us standing next to one another with a smile. He compared them to the photos on my Facebook then, and expressed how happy I looked with him and how miserable I now looked on Facebook.

Leo knew he was not getting through to him and saw the intensity that I had expressed about him in the past. Leo warned me on the voice message to maybe not stay home alone tonight, as he said this guy was going to stop by with a gift for me.

This was Christmas Eve. I was not home that night because of my work. The "nice" Connie was no longer going to tolerate this behavior. I was now angry. Angry that he would bother MY friends and use them to get to me. He crossed the line.

On Christmas morning, I was still at my client's home as I knew he had only hours to live. This wonderful soul was ninety-one and ready to transition.

His wife had said to him, "You better stick around and not ruin our Christmas." They were married over sixty-five years.

Once my client was comfortable and had his meds on board, I took a few minutes to send out a text to what had now become some stalker-like guy. It read, "LEAVE MY FRIENDS ALONE!"

The banter back and forth for the next twenty to thirty minutes was extremely frustrating. I knew that my patient's two daughters, son, wife, and grandkids were going to be losing this man—their dad, husband, grandfather, and friend. Meanwhile, here I was dealing with what I then called a nut.

Each short sentence I wrote was capitalized. My last one to him was, "STOP TEXTING ME! LEAVE ME ALONE!" That didn't stop him. I just put my phone away, but I knew I needed to do something more.

The next few hours were all about my patient. He passed peacefully at 4:30 p.m. on Christmas Day, surrounded by his family. It was his time to transition.

After his body was removed from the house, I gave his wife a hug and went home. I was exhausted, drained in many ways from being in the energy of so much heartache, and yet I always feel blessed to have the pleasure of being part of anyone's transition.

It's truly an honor.

The next day, I called my good friend Gerry, a retired police officer and detective. His last four years on the job were as the Union President, a job he didn't mind leaving behind. I asked him if he would come with me to my local town police station in Needham. Gerry would do anything for me, and he knows I would do the same for him. He's become a good friend over the years. I know his entire family and have spent many holidays with them. His mom is my movie date on Saturday nights sometimes. She's one of my favorite people on the planet, ninety-four years young.

Gerry accompanied me to the station. The police officer I spoke to didn't need many details as he could hear and see in my voice the anger, fear, and frustration I was having just talking about the "nut". I asked the officer if he would call this man and ask him to leave me alone. They were happy to do that.

I got a call later that afternoon from the officer saying they reached the man in question. He had told the officer he had a gift for me. The officer told him to stay away from me and not go to my home. The officer called me later that afternoon and told me, "You should be all set. He should leave you alone, but if you hear from him again, please call us back." I felt a huge relief. It was over, and he would now leave me alone.

Ten days later, during a snowstorm, this relentless soul drove fifty to sixty miles to my home. His footprints were in the snow. The gift in the brown box he'd left was not addressed and had no return label, and no card, but it was camera equipment, and I knew it was from him.

I felt scared in my own home for the first time. I felt like it was not safe there and that he did not listen to me or the Needham Police. I wondered what he was capable of.

I called the police, and they suggested I go to the courthouse and get a restraining order. I had never been to a courthouse for myself before. I had never stood in front of a judge. I had never requested a restraining order. It was all so foreign to me.

Gerry was again by my side. I sat there most of the morning waiting for my name to be called, and eventually it was. As I stood in front of the judge, I was nervous. He asked me a few pointed questions. One I remember was, "What does this man do for a living?" The judge seemed to be on his side when I told him he was a pharmacist, which made no sense to me.

I asked the judge three times, "How can I protect myself from him?" He was unable to give me an answer and continued to side with him. It was not what I expected. I learned that I was welcome back the following Thursday with the man in question. I asked if they would invite him, and I was told "yes". I left there feeling powerless, but hopeful that I may have better results the following week.

As I met with Gerry again that next Thursday morning, I had an interesting thought that I shared with him. I had purchased one, and only one, gift for this man in the few months we were dating.

It was a black Tommy Hilfiger sweater with a zipper down to the breastbone. I said to Gerry, "I'll bet he'll be wearing it." And sure enough, he walked into the courtroom fifteen minutes late wearing that sweater.

Another good friend, PJ, reminded me that he had a similar court experience with a woman. "This is like a date for them, being in the same building with the person they're obsessed with."

We were both called to stand in front of the same judge. I was not very hopeful as I felt the judge would again take his side, given his appearance and how he had a good job. None of this erased my fear of him.

The judge gave him time to read the request for a restraining order I had put together, and then asked him what he did for work. He also asked, "Are you going to leave this girl alone?" Then the judge turned to me and said, "He said he will leave you alone" and denied the restraining order.

I have a better understanding of the situation now: one must have their life *threatened* to obtain a restraining order and since he hadn't threatened my life, no order could be issued. But I was afraid of him not listening to me or the police and I said to the judge, "No offense, your honor, but I don't think he will listen to you either." The judge seemed content nonetheless that he had said he would leave me alone.

That was not good enough for me. He had not listened to the police when they requested that he stay away from me.

I asked the judge again, "How can I protect myself?" He said, "Well, I'm not telling you what to do, but you could look into getting a harassment order." It turned out to be the EXACT SAME PAPERWORK. The only difference was that I was requesting a harassment order and not a restraining order.

Back I went into the courtroom with the new paperwork waiting to be called, but they broke for lunch instead. So, back again that afternoon, in front of the same judge. The day seemed endless. Being in that energy all day was not fun.

When requesting a harassment order, one needs to present three pieces of evidence indicating the harassment. Luckily, I had done my homework and brought with me several pieces of evidence, in case they might be needed: relentless texts and scary emails from him.

When our names were called, we went to a different room, in front of a different judge, and started over. I didn't know if this would help me or hurt me, but I had no choice.

As I stood in front of this new judge, I was talking a mile a minute until he nicely said, "Slow down, slow down," with a warm smile on his face and a mustache curled up to his cheeks. He was much kinder, even his facial expression was more relaxing. He took a few moments and read more than three different proofs of harassment that I'd brought.

I had also provided the judge with other pieces of information about this guy, such as that he had a gun and a license to carry it and a prior restraining order from his wife.

The judge asked him, "Why didn't you leave her alone? Why didn't you listen to the Needham Police?"

All he said was, "I will leave her alone."

Clearly the judge was on my side, and I was granted the harassment order, as of that day, for three months.

I got immediate protection. We were no longer allowed to be in the same room, and I had to leave the building before he could leave that room. Walking out of the courthouse, I felt confident. I finally felt I'd been heard. I felt validated and I also think that guy—the defendant—finally heard the words "Leave her alone."

I've never seen or heard from that guy since.

Thank God!

MAMMY'S PASSING

"PLEASE READ IF YOU HAVE NOT MET ME

My name is Mary. I'm very compliant and I love to sing. I will not tell you I'm thirsty, so please ask me. I enjoy sips of water and more so 7-Up throughout the day and in the middle of the night when I'm awake.

My lower back usually hurts and I need a pillow to support it.

I will not complain of pain or hunger, so please ask me. I like to be kept warm.

I don't always remember where I am, but I'm comforted to know I'm in a hospital setting.

(I don't understand the difference between hospice and hospital.)

MEALS: Don't trust me to eat by myself—I sometimes put an empty fork to my mouth, so if my family are not here, I will need help.

I don't like pasta, cheese, or yogurt . . . bread sometimes, but it can make me cough more . . .

But a little brown bread with butter if I feel like it, is yummy.

I do like soft food. Hard food can be difficult to chew at times. I like veg soup,

chicken, veggies, mashed potatoes with butter, jelly, ice cream, custard, and apple pie.

I like to wear an inside shirt with my nighty—and always a robe when I'm sitting out.

I love to smile. I cry sometimes and I'm confused a lot of the time. I love a visit from the priest. Trish Burke gave me an amazing Jacuzzi and I was excited to know I can be taken to a Catholic Mass.

I respond well to smiles and the energy of love.

My heart is filled with only love.

Thank you for reading this . . ."

This was a note posted in Mammy's hospice room.

St. Theresa's was a ward at the Regional Hospital in Galway, where my mom would be for the next three months. Daily visits from my family kept her company. Her mind was not the same, her walls of defense were down, and she became more loving, and sweet.

She was thirty pounds lighter, but the same smile and eyes awaited my visits. Each day, I would sit with her for close to twelve hours. I knew she was not capable of asking for what she needed, or to know what she wanted. Twice she didn't even notice that she had not urinated for hours, and I would inform the nurse. The tests they did validated that her bladder was full. Time to catheterize her, to release the fluid. The second time, I informed them they'd left it in.

I often still wonder, "When would they have noticed?" My mom's dementia was wide awake and not going back to sleep.

She had no concept of time and didn't understand why she couldn't walk anymore. Her back pain returned and there was very little relief. They also found traces of cancer in an ulcer, but it would have required surgery to have it biopsied, and we knew she would not be able to handle that.

We got her on board with the palliative care team to treat the pain, as we'd done with my dad years earlier. It was Christmastime, so she stayed in the hospital over Christmas, awaiting a bed at the beautiful Galway Hospice.

◦ ◦ ◦

Will this be the last time I see her alive?

That was my thought each trip I made home from December 2015 to June 2016.

I would check in with Laura, my energy healer, who's got mediumship abilities and has often shared her thoughts with me when someone is going to pass.

Each time I would return from Ireland, Laura would reassure me. "You will see her again." This was hard to believe, as my mom continued to decline after each stroke. The fifth trip in that seventh month would be the last time I'd see her alive.

I was anxious as she continued to decline. I'd check in with Laura, asking if I should move my trip up and go sooner. She'd ask, "What date are you going?"

It would be for her eighty-fourth birthday, and I would be there a few days prior. Laura told me with confidence that I would be in the country, but not in the room with her, as she wanted to pass in the energy of males.

The bad turn or stroke she got the morning I landed was the one that moved her future away from us and closer to God.

It was a Tuesday. She was no longer eating, she drank very little, and she slept a lot. I decided to stay with her the last two nights she remained on earth so she was not alone.

The caregivers checked on her every two to three hours, which was very comforting. It was a Friday, and her breath became labored. My brothers were in and out most of the days. She'd take several deep breaths, then hold each one for twenty seconds or longer, and each time they were thinking, "This will be the last one." This continued on and off for the next twenty-four hours.

In Ireland, the family of the deceased wear tuxedos at the wake and funeral (a great business for clothing rental stores). It was Saturday. I was surprised Mammy was still with us, given her condition the night before. She was much more at peace and was calm. Sunday, the stores would be closed, and Monday was a holiday. The tuxedos needed to be picked up today.

My sister and I decided we could pick up the few suits we needed and shoes. We knew all the sizes. I asked my sister, "Are you OK if she passes when we are out?" She said she was. We both had done as much as we could for Mammy and knew she was pain-free and safe.

Laura was right about Mammy transitioning in the energy of males. There were five of them around her when she was taken home to God.

° ° °

As my dad often said, "If you live long enough, you'll be once a man and twice a child." Mammy had also become a child again.

In addition to the many pajamas I would bring to Ireland from America, one of my visits yo Mammy included an activity blanket and a doll. The doll wore a navy-and white-striped dress, with two cherries on the front. The doll's arms and legs were pale blue, and her hair was black, with red ribbons tied around two pigtails. Mammy loved to undress her.

The doll was her favorite and it stood out beside the many stuffed animals that kept her company at night.

A longstanding tradition in Ireland, is that when a body is waked at home, it should never be left alone. Willie, my sister's good neighbor, was the man who offered to sit with Daddy when he was waked. He offered again for Mammy. He sat beside them all night, until the body was taken out and brought to the church.

The first wake was held at my sister's house, and the second wake occurred in the church.

Mammy was laid out in comfortable attire, wearing a purple Pashmina scarf wrapped loosely around her neck. Before we closed the lid on Mammy's coffin for the last time—like with Daddy's whistle—my sister and I made sure to place her favorite doll next to her to keep her company so she didn't feel alone.

As the undertaker brought my mom to my sister's home for the first wake, we were greeted by the villagers who were alongside the road. They had small, makeshift altars set next to them, with blessed candles flickering, and the people blessed themselves.

It was a cold June day, a cloudy day, and the wind was blowing.

◦ ◦ ◦

My Facebook post from that day:

> *"It is with a heavy heart, deep sadness, and immense appreciation to the staff at the University Hospital, Galway, Galway Hospice;, and all the team/staff members at Corrandulla Nursing Home, for caring with such compassion for my Mother, Mary McNamara, who transitioned this evening.*
>
> *My Mom's been a resident over the past several months at Corrandulla Nursing Home. She passed away today on the eve of her 84th birthday very peacefully, thanks to the Palliative Care Team who have hovered over her since December.*
>
> *She's been a real trooper as her body became fragile and her muscles deconditioned, and her memory journeyed elsewhere, but her spirit shone brighter than ever before.*
>
> *My mom transitioned into the beautiful soul God had intended her to be. As her dementia awakened so did her bright soul.*
>
> *We will celebrate with her body tomorrow while her soul dances with my dad's and my sister's . . . R.I.P Mammy . . . we miss you and love you. Happy Birthday . . . and thank you for the gift of life!"*

◦ ◦ ◦

We had pure, unconditional love between each other when I went into her world of dementia. I sat with her ten to twelve hours each day. I couldn't get enough of her. Most of this time was in silence or, as some would call it, “a state of confusion.” It might’ve sounded confusing if one only listened to her words, but she always made sense to me as I journeyed with her.

There were many amazing moments of “connections” that linked us together, tightening the bonds between us, mother and daughter, and I will cherish those until I take my last breath and we reunite again.

In some moments each day, I could have been her daughter, mother, doctor, neighbor, or nurse. I would wear whichever “hat” she placed on me in any given hour or moment.

Her laughter was adorable. When she’d say something and quickly realize she should not have said it, she’d make the same gesture as a child would when they knew they did something wrong: her mouth would open to the letter “O,” and she’d cover it with her hand. This always brought a big smile to my face. She’d see it in my eyes and smile back because she knew she’d done nothing wrong.

It became impossible for her to do or say anything wrong. The only time I’d correct her or guide her, was when she was scared or judging herself in a negative light.

The messages she fed herself over the years were still playing softly in the background of the awakened part of her brain from the past. “I’m stupid, I can’t spell very well, I had no education.” Yet she was loyal and true to her partner of almost fifty years, and she survived six births with no painkillers, the death of her first daughter, the death of her first grandchild, and at least one miscarriage.

She quit smoking as soon as she was pregnant. She knew she was pregnant when she lit a cigarette one morning. It became a disgusting taste to her. That was the pregnancy test.

Not only was he not present when his children were born, but Daddy stayed clear of us for the entire first year. He thought we might break, like china dolls, and back then it was a woman's job to change the diapers.

They were cloth diapers, as well. It was her job to wash, dry, and recycle them. The clothesline was usually full on the days there was a "good drying out," but one would always have to keep an eye out for the rain showers, which sometimes came on suddenly.

Empathy for my mom triggered something in me, or was it a miracle? It came from someplace inside me, a place in the core of my being from which I was able to forgive.

It happened over many hours of just sitting next to Mom's bedside. It was in December, six months before my mom transitioned. The Mom I had known, and only visited from time to time, now had dementia that took her into a different world. It was a world I am familiar with from the years I worked in homecare. I learned how to go into that world a long time ago, as I knew people were no longer able to come into mine.

I was always at the hospital at 8 a.m., early enough to chat with my mom's caregiver before she left, so I would hear directly from her how she got through the night. My mom was in a section of a big ward that was separated in part from the other patients.

I would joke with her and tell her she was one of the troublemakers. There were four of them that needed what was called a "Carer" overnight to keep an additional eye on them.

One lady in her nineties was a wanderer and a fall risk. The others, including my mom, were confined to their beds and were unable to ask for help when they needed a drink or to use the bathroom.

o o o

My Tribute to Mammy

"For those of you who don't know me, I am the youngest of five children, and so I was my parents' birth-control, as I had to share a bed with them for the first 12 years of my life in that lovely thatched house that was built in 1840.

As a child, one of my favorite places to hide or hang out was up in the apple tree . . . no one knew I was there, the leaves covered me and the chair I was sitting on. I would hear my name Con-cep-ta being called many times throughout the day and I would just sit quietly.

I knew by the time I returned home, Mammy would forget what she wanted me for, or someone else got the job.

Given my mom's amazing entrance into this world back in 1933, with her twin brother Paddy, both together weighing 3 pounds total weight, they were miracle babies. No incubators, no early intervention. She had very little education, but was one hell of a knitter, and she made the best white scones.

Her sisters both live in Boston, Della and Terry, and growing up they used to hear the knitting needles clinging together even in the dark . . . and she's often said over the years, 'Sure, I could knit that with my eyes closed' and she could, eyes closed or in the dark—and never followed a pattern. But even without a great education she would go on to teach us many life lessons.

She would often say, 'Go outside and put up a jump for yourself'—that taught me how to be independent. "Make yourself useful" was another one of her great sayings. That taught me how to engage with others. And of course, the one we've all heard, 'Stop crying or I will give you something to cry about' . . . this helped me to express my needs verbally.

For the first five years after I left home, my conversations with my mom were at our neighbors' house, the Concanons, as we didn't have a landline, not to mention a cell phone.

The first call to the Concanons would be, 'Can you please ask Mammy to be at your house and I will call back in an hour?' On the second call, she was always at the other end of the phone, eager as I was, to hear one another's voice. It was seven years before I came back home to visit for the first time . . . that was the year I got my green card, and I've been home every year since.

The visits became so frequent and the phone calls were so often, I sometimes would get, 'Oh hello, Connie, "My Fair City" just started, can you call me later?' . . . or sometimes, it was 'Murder She Wrote . . .

Each year my visit would consist of many cups of tea and chats with her, sometimes another sweater made, lunch or food shopping, or just hanging out around the fire telling stories. Her many visits to the US were always a great conversation piece.

This past December, I came home to a different lady. I asked her, 'Who are you and what did you do with my mom?' She would always smile, didn't always remember if she was my mother or if I was hers—she didn't always make sense as her dementia was wide awake. The many, many fun chats we had over the three weeks I was here were truly priceless.

As I entered her world—the one she was living in—it could be a very fun place at times, most of the time . . . and when it was scary, I would make sure she knew she was safe.

Mammy was no longer able to stay present in my world, so I went into hers, and I was always welcome.

Some days I was her mom, her nurse, her doctor . . . and once in a while I was her daughter, other times she would tell me about her daughter Connie who lived in America and I would always say, 'I heard she's very nice' . . . she always agreed and followed with a smile.

The few short weeks I was here, I was able to be by her side. Each morning, as her eyes would open, mine would be there to greet her, followed by a two-way smile.

Her day always had a verse or two of songs. 'Never Grow Old' and 'Three Leaf Shamrock were her favorite hits. She sang for the nurses and the doctors, and even Father McNamara got to enjoy it.

The Palliative Care team took her under their wing, which led us to the Galway Hospice. From the day of admission, a team of angels flocked around her, day and night, making sure her needs were met from all aspects. Angel Trish gave her her first Jacuzzi. We both got to enjoy her sitting back in a room with dim candlelight and soft music, and we chose for her the color purple to light up the water.

She was then transitioned to the 'penthouse suite' at Corrandulla Nursing Home. The staff welcomed her and took excellent care of her . . . and much appreciation to the entire staff at the nursing home—from the people who opened the door for us, to the ones who made sure my Mom was comfortable, and everyone in between, too many to mention. Each one brought their own flavor of care, concern, and love with them as they engaged with my Mom.

And of course, her most regular visitor, Robert, Noreen's husband—even stayed next to her some nights . . . two beautiful souls connecting through their silence and dementia—powerful and not quite understood from our everyday, limited minds.

My sister, brothers, and their families were there every day. I heard about the

neighbors who stopped in to make sure she was also loved and not forgotten . . . her mind may not have remembered you were there, but her soul was engaged with yours.

Before my final visit, and thanks to technology, my interactions with her were through video where I could still see those beautiful eyes and smile as her body grew old—I got daily updates, morning and evening, which helped me feel closer to her.

I will be forever grateful for the gifts that our souls gave to one another in these past few months. She has transitioned to the land where her soul will never grow old—and many leaves of shamrock will be growing next to her resting place.

I will miss her smiling face and blue eyes, as her soul now resides in my heart, alongside Daddy. Thank you on behalf of Gerry, Johnny, Patsy, Noreen, and myself for giving us life.

Until we meet again—God Bless, Namaste."

° ° °

Walking through the grocery store one week before the eighth month anniversary of my mom's passing, I thought back to one of the few times I experienced her choking on a piece of bread that she craved.

The tears were running down my cheeks. Luckily, I had my sunglasses with me on that winter day.

I knew when I got in my car it would be a safe place to cry as loudly as I needed to. It helped when I reached out to my sister in Ireland. She had to struggle some days with her sense of loss also.

It's still a comfort to relive stories about Mammy with my sister today.

Mammy and Me

THE BLOCK

In March 2016, I convinced my good friend Gene to join me on a day trip to Block Island, otherwise known as "the Block."

He lived in Rhode Island, so I left my car there and we took his. Driver, his beloved Golden Retriever, was with us.

The "boat," as the Islanders call it—what the rest of us called the Ferry—departed on time from Point Judith, RI. We were dressed for a cold day and sat on the upper deck outside so Driver could enjoy the fresh air also.

The round trip was around $80 for the car and $20 per person. Driver was free. As we drove off the boat, we had no idea whether we should take a left or a right and we didn't really care. We had three hours before the boat would take us back. Our bellies were hungry, and the only restaurant open during the day was in front of us, so we decided to stop for a bite to eat at the Mohegan Cafe and Brewery.

I don't remember what I ordered, but I remember the friendly waiter and the man we met, with whom we're still good friends today.

Gene talks on the loud side, and the restaurant was empty. It was clear we were strangers to the Island. To this day, I would say the most knowledgeable man on the Island happened to be having lunch a few seats away from us.

Coincidence, or were we meant to meet?

Given that I believe the people who are supposed to be in your life, will enter when they are supposed to, today it was Bob: Robert J. Rule.

Bob decided to leave his warm home and get lunch in the town. He asked if we would like a few suggestions, having overheard our banter. He told us where to go, and what to see, for the couple of hours we had left.

I learned later that the "transfer station" is the dump, and that was one of the places Bob had suggested we check out. Not the dump itself, but the beach on the other side of it. He suggested we take a right at the "DUMP" sign, but I also asked where the best place was to capture a sunset on Block Island.

Without hesitation, he answered, "My house." My next question, of course, being Irish, was, "Do you have teabags?" He said he did, but he didn't know how fresh they were. He said he wasn't a caffeine drinker and not a tea or coffee man.

The twenty- to thirty-minute chat led to us exchanging business cards, and he also invited me, Gene (and Driver) to come to his home anytime we wanted. "It sleeps nine guests," he added. Gene was not sure about this guy, but being Irish I know he was, in part, like a good Irishman: friendly, kind, and helpful, with no agenda. Just the goodness of his heart.

We got a little lost and only saw one beach, and stone walls like the ones back home in Ireland. I got a feel for the place and wanted to return soon. I use the word "lost" loosely, as it's impossible to get lost on the Block, but we didn't know where we were. The island is only seven miles by three.

Bob informed us that eight hundred residents live there all year round, he being one of them.

I felt safe in Bob's energy and I also felt I was making a new friend. Little did I know that day how the next year or two would unfold, and how our friendship would deepen and remain intact today.

A week or two went by, and Bob and I were on the phone talking and listening to one another's stories, like we knew each other from another lifetime, like our souls had connected before. The ease of banter back and forth was welcoming on both parts. Bob assumed Gene and I were a couple, so when he invited me to come visit, he assumed Driver and his "dad" would be with me.

The time came when the Block called to me again. This time it would be for a weekend. Bob extended an invitation to me and anyone else I chose to bring along.

In turn, I extended an invitation to a couple I knew who had invited me to North Conway, NH the prior weekend. They were to meet me at Point Judith Friday evening to catch the boat. I also asked my good friend Jimmy, a photographer who works in the forensic unit of the Boston Police Department. He was supposed to come on Saturday.

I remember it like it was yesterday, driving to Point Judith alone, after learning my friends had to cancel last minute. Chatting with Gene, as I often still do, I joked and said, "Hey, if you don't hear from me after this weekend, assume that Bob kidnapped me."

I had a smile ear-to-ear as I was saying this, and I knew in my heart of hearts there wasn't a bad bone in Bob's body, an expression my mom would often use. My mom was fond of everyone. My dad was more honest.

A memory I really like and often repeat to friends, was when my mom would come home from a wake and say, "How lovely the corpse looked and how he was such a nice man." But, if my dad had a grudge towards him, and didn't like him in waking life, he would say, "He was a bastard when he was alive and he's still a bastard now that he's dead." That would be followed by Mammy blessing herself, not sure if she were praying for the deceased or my dad. Maybe both.

I loved his brutal honesty. You always knew where you stood with my dad.

Bob was waiting at the dock for me with a big smile and huge enthusiasm. To this day, he is the best and most knowledgeable tour guide on the Block. It helps that he was a history teacher. He frequents symposiums in New York City and was a teacher at Manhasset High School in New York.

He is also the inventor of the modern Lacrosse stick and, I believe a glove design, with patents hanging on his wall. Bob was a highly successful lacrosse coach and remains in touch to this day with fellow coaches and players.

That first of many weekends at Bob's was filled with adventure, many walks, lots of chat, and good food. I drifted off to sleep that first night in what is now called "Concepta's Room" with the sliding glass doors open, listening to what has become one of my favorite tunes, the buoy bell in the distance, clanging in the wind, a measured, meditative sound between the wrestling ocean waves and momentary calms.

I'm not a big fan of the ocean, when I have to travel on it. It has a mind of its own. But it's one of my favorite places to be next to, when I am on solid ground.

During that weekend we cooked in and ate out. It was now summertime, and Block Island was wide awake. To this day, the best place to take a nap is on Bob's hammock, or if it's on the chilly side, his large windowsill where the warm sun often shines through.

The shops, restaurants, churches, and lighthouses we saw, were all full of life. Most of the walks were on private property, but that didn't mean "stay off," or at least we didn't read it as that.

The driveway to Bob's house has only room for one car and deer crossings. At home in Ireland, it would be called a *boreen*, for sure.

Sunday morning, as I slowly awakened to the birds chirping, it was time to return to Boston. The first words out of Bob's mouth that morning were, "I want you to know you are welcome here anytime, even when I'm not here." I said, "I would love to come back, to see what it's like in all seasons."

I felt what he said was sincere, as he is a sincere soul. After breakfast he took me to the "boat." I wanted to sound like an Islander and not call it the ferry.

Fifty minutes later, I was in my car with an hour and a half drive ahead. I called Gene to let him know Bob didn't kidnap me and I shared with him the wonderful experience I had. I had my camera on all my walks, so I also captured many beautiful pictures. At the time, what I was looking at looked like images of Ireland.

As I edited the photos over the following days, I got to relive those great experiences. I also wanted to do something nice as a token of my appreciation for Bob, and a coffee table photo book came to mind. I had taken pictures of him sitting on a rock, on one of the beaches, and looking through his binoculars. I gave those photos, and others, to him in a book with the title "Another Day at the Office for Bob."

He was touched and delighted with the thoughtful gift.

This gift inspired him as he was lying awake one night, thinking about my creativity with the book, and my wanting to come back every season. His business mind was awake. Later he was excited about sharing a fun project we could do together.

His idea was to create a book of the four seasons on the Block. It is now a coffee table book, titled *Seasons on the Block*, currently on sale at the Glasswork Onion and Historical Society.

It was a fun year of back and forth to the Block to make it. Bob was always game to capture another sunset. He will also get up at 4 a.m. to capture a sunrise, even in the snow.

The flights from Westerly Airport are more reliable and much faster than the boat. The flight is only ten minutes to the Block. Most of the time, I get to be the co-pilot. Linda, the pilot with the long braid, is the most fun and engaging.

One of the stories she shared with me was about the day she was bringing food from the airport to the Island. One can have a pizza delivered if the plane is going. The story was not about a pizza, but it was about live lobsters that were in the back seat of the aircraft, the bag clearly not tied properly. The lobsters escaped, crawling around Linda's feet. She calmly returned them to their bag when she landed. I made a fun movie for her once, of her landing in slow motion.

Another one of my fun shoots on the Block was from a helicopter. It was designed for photographers, in my opinion, as it had no glass. I got to sit up front with the pilot, who was also a photographer, and he knew a great spot to shoot: an aerial view of the towering windmills located three miles off the coast of the island, floating on the ocean. These also made it into my *Seasons* book.

In the summer, some of the places we frequent are The Oar, Dead Eye Dick's, and Poor Man's Pub. Ballard's is my favorite for breakfast, with patio seating overlooking the beach. Other favorites are The Atlantic Inn, The Barn, or The Diner in the winter season.

I also got to experience the 4th of July there in 2016. It was so friendly and spectacular. We hung out on the beach, with lots of bug spray, and I captured some great shots without my tripod. The reflections off the water were an added treat.

The sunset was also breathtaking the next night. It was another picture that made it into my book.

Bob and I will always remain friends and I continue to accept his open invitation. Not as much in the winter, but summer and fall I will be there, discovering new walks with him, even if they are not paved.

Bob has a way of making this happen.

MIND AND MASSAGE

I have always worked with people, in nursing homes and private homes, providing care directly or supervising the care.

I got it into my head that I wanted to be a massage therapist and opted to take the route of a one-year program at Spa Tech Institute, Westborough, MA in 2004.

It was a very busy year, as I was working full-time and in school three evenings a week. Eventually, the clinical work was done on Saturdays, which used to be my day off. I knew it would not be forever. I went into every exam thinking I would fail, but I didn't. I was very good at the hands-on and demo work, but less so with a written exam. Those will never be my first choice.

The good part about the location I chose to get my education, was that it was west of where I lived. In the evening, I was driving against the traffic. At night, coming home was traffic-free for the most part, except for the construction often found on Route 128.

I enjoyed learning about the body. It was a very personal challenge, allowing different people to touch me, and me them, when working on each other's bodies.

It took many years of therapy to have my body react to normal touch. My body never seemed to recognize what a safe touch was, one of the many scars that come with being sexually abused.

I knew I was ready and felt mentally strong enough to handle any triggers if they would emerge. I also enjoy being in the safe touch that my body receives during a massage session, or Reiki.

A frightened soul seems to relax easily in my company. I've been told that I have a "disarming", natural ability. The room I work in is also a very safe space where I allow people to bring their complete body, mind, and soul with them.

I do suggest that they leave the traffic behind, that they have been sitting in for the past twenty to thirty minutes. Some feel the need to bring their boss with them—figuratively—but, after a few sentences, I try to have them become present, unless I feel that they need to vent longer. It's rewarding to be able to see the transformation and how differently (and better) they feel after fifty minutes.

I sometimes share nuggets of wisdom that can be life changing, or as Oprah would say, "a light-bulb moment" or an "Aha!" moment.

It amazes me how a stranger can walk through my door and five or ten minutes later, they'd be lying naked on my table. They are under the covers, of course, and some do leave their underwear on as it's more comfortable for them.

Understanding that the glutes hold great tension, and that they're sat on through most people's day, I have a different way of seeing them: They are an extension of the legs.

I always suggest, if the client is comfortable, disrobing completely so I can work on the gluteus maximus, particularly if there are sciatic issues. I will not personally get a massage from any therapist who will not work those muscles, and I know many don't. I have a hard time understanding this.

I make sure the client always feels secure when I drape them. Many clients feel comfortable in their head, but their body is not. It's so beautiful to see a scared, tense, tightly wrapped body let go. It's a combination of safe touch, correct pressure, and, to a greater degree, the energy from me and my space that frees them.

In the cooler weather, my table is heated with an electric fire flickering, as much for my own comfort and peace of mind, as for my clients. I usually have a different scent being diffused to add to the calm atmosphere. Lemongrass is a favorite and I will often add a little peppermint, lavender, or even lemon to it. This often helps people become present, as well. Their mind gets triggered, and their senses become present. Peppermint also keeps the nasal passages from clogging up.

I always invite the client to check in with their body, to know if we should start supine or prone. Many will say, "I don't know, what do you think?" This is where I will invite them again to check in with their body and I will add, "What feels achy or what feels like it needs more attention. Neck, shoulders, back, feet?" This usually helps them become a little more present in their body.

Many times, I must ask twice as they want to be told what to do and don't always know how to check in, without guidance. They learn quickly; usually on the next visit they will start with something like, "My neck hurts today, so I will start on my back, face up."

When we have determined what would be the best way to start, I will leave the room until they get settled in. Some clients don't want to leave their mind and that may be why they need to talk throughout the session. Some people are not capable of leaving their mind, while others carry pain in their body and use up most of their energy trying to control it. I try to invite most clients to be present. Still, some people who have no one to vent to, or who carry great anxiety, feel more relaxed when they're talking.

I have a thriving massage practice. I care about all my clients and even have love for many of them. I also perform Reiki on my more open-minded clients. More than sore muscles get released using this technique, beyond just the stress or tension.

"Stuck" energy can be released when a client's body is ready. I love when I see a client for the third or fourth time and they say, "Wow, that felt so amazing. What did you do differently?" I smile and share with them that their body was more receptive to releasing tension.

I will always remember a story my cousin shared with me about one of her many trips to Disney World. She had booked a massage treatment at her hotel and shared with the therapist that she'd been on her feet all day and that they really ached.

She was the owner of a massage practice here in Boston and became very familiar with her body and how it liked to be touched.

She was so disappointed with the massage therapist there, who spent only the last five minutes of treatment on her feet, at the end of the session.

That would be a cue for me as to where to start.

Educating the client is part of my practice, reminding them to voice their needs during a massage, especially if their needs are not being met. This is beneficial to both the massage therapist and client, leading to a more effective treatment.

I try to be available 11 a.m. to 7 p.m. to provide massage and Reiki sessions. The earliest I like to start my workday is 11 a.m., as I love the morning to myself. I hit the gym and in the nicer weather, I will hike Wilson Mountain also. People who do advanced hikes call it a pimple. To me, it's a great way to spend forty-five minutes in nature, with blue or red paint on the trees to keep me on track, and I like to follow the blue. They knew I would get lost otherwise.

My clients book either a fifty- or eighty-minute session and some ask for ninety minutes. I personally prefer a ninety-minute massage, as fifty is way too short for a full-body massage. If I only have fifty minutes, I will have my therapist focus on two different areas: neck & shoulders, and back & glutes.

Some of my massage clients are the most stressed souls.

Some carry too much adipose tissue as a result and have sore hips and knees, and they usually have an unhealthy relationship with food, by overeating.

One lady that I met was the opposite. She needed food but she needed to keep her food down and not purge. A beautiful soul, but she was out of control with her eating and purging. She was a psychotherapist, as well.

I rarely share my personal past with my clients, but I felt compelled to do so with her.

I stepped out of the room while she was getting comfortable under the cover of the warm table, and I quietly asked God to "help me" or "use me" during the next fifty minutes. This is not the first anorexic/bulimic client I have worked on, but the first one I felt I needed to talk with and engage.

I asked her what pressure she would like, or was used to, and I included "as you have very little muscle to work on." I never judge the body I'm working on aloud. Many bodies are carrying more weight than is healthy, but I keep that to myself.

I'm also aware that the body may be carrying many secrets.

As I cupped her neck in my hands, I knew one hand would be enough, as her neck and body were emaciated. Her face looked too big for her body. I felt compelled to say more. I listened to her open up with tears flowing down her face, and I shared part of my own story. The addiction and eating disorder parts. Our connection deepened, and it was clear that she was out of control.

She battled for fifteen years with this heartbreaking illness, from eating out of dumpsters, to working out for hours. I made a deal with her: If she called my former therapist, I would give her a complimentary Reiki session. She agreed without hesitation.

My therapist, Dr. Fanger, refused to work with her. He talked with her for twenty to thirty minutes, but learned she needed hospitalization and not out-patient therapy.

She was too sick. She hung up from the call and continued to eat and purge.

Reiki was the only modality she had not tried for her disorder. She needs far more than a Reiki session, but potentially it could awaken more of her desire to get better. But, she felt too ashamed to return after that one session.

She's been a hospital inpatient and has seen, in her words, "every eating disorder therapist and specialist in her area." It seems their behaviors or styles don't reach her, or she was not ready, or maybe it was because of her insurance, who knows. She did say her mom would sell her house to help her.

She loves her mom. Her mom was her "everything," but now all they do is fight, and her mom is afraid of losing her. And food is a big topic for them.

I got a call from her mom, saying she finally accepted help again. She will be an inpatient hopefully for the next few months, God willing. It made my day to learn she was at desperation's door again and open to help.

She doesn't have a spiritual practice. It was one of the questions I asked her five minutes into our session. I suggested she borrow my God. I even said a prayer out loud for her. I suggested, and will continue suggesting, that while she's on her knees purging, to ask God/Higher Power/Source for help.

Before closing my eyes that night, I sent a message to my brother in Ireland to light a blessed candle. All I have here are the Yankee candles. I'm assuming the blessed ones are more powerful.

My next thought, before I drifted off to sleep, was to reach out to Dr. Phil, on her behalf, as he is who I unwind with some evenings. I have seen him help the sickest, most lost souls. I sent him three or four emails, as they only allow 250 words. I'm sure my emails are among millions, but I have faith.

Unfortunately, Dr. Fanger will not see her without having six months of "sobriety" with her food. Therapy would not be effective while her eating disorder is still active. When I told her about the candle, I sent her a photo of it after my brother sent it to me. She was so touched and said she will print it and hang it in her room/office. Maybe the faith is starting to build.

I believe and trust that a small part of her wants help, and like a drunk she wants to get well without giving up the purging. I wanted to get well without giving up drinking. Impossible.

Her lack of honesty is what sticks out the most to me. I don't think she's been able to maintain healthy eating long enough to do any work, so she's on the road to her death.

Gratitude poured over me to have been blessed with the gift of desperation, to be willing to deal with the underlying causes that my own purging masked.

I hope one day she comes back to claim the Reiki session I offered her.

LIGHT

My passion, my calling, is to help people awaken, from the inside out.

My good pal, Dr. Wayne Dyer—not really a pal, I just like to think of him that way—has created so many wise one-liners that live with me daily. One of them is, "When we change the way we look at things, things change."

When I first got sober, he was the only man I trusted. I bought all his books and if they were available via CD, I would get them in that version also. It was as if he was talking just to me, and I was holding on to every word.

My own thinking was extremely distorted and a dark place to be alone. Getting sober was not too difficult for me, although it helped that I was not yet addicted to it physically, only emotionally. I never reached the point of having the shakes or withdrawals that I learned about over the first year in the AA program.

Getting sober was the easy part. *Staying* sober was the hard part. It was easy the first few days as I was so sick and tired of doing the same thing over and over again expecting different results. The jig was up. I didn't know that then. I will forever be grateful to God for the gift of sobriety.

I have always been a solutions-minded person when I can be. I will spend ten minutes on a problem and ten hours on a solution if needs be. I have given suggestions and have been an ear for a few family members and friends over the years.

Some of my chats with them would be, "File this away, as you may need it one day," or, "File this as 'just data' for now." The younger ones did need to file the info away until it sank in, and two of them told me the same thing a few years ago when they were in their twenties: "Now I know what you meant."

Our minds are powerful. That is the good news and the bad news. When it's directed toward our highest good, it's a source of power, but when it's operating from fear and obsession, it is a painful place.

Our minds lie to us. The mind can be very limiting when we only see one dimension. When we add our gut instincts, thoughts, intuition, and wisdom, as well as our other senses, we can change the entire picture. It allows more data in, and it can change everything.

Our inner child also gets to see it through his or her eyes. If our early childhood was compromised, it will be seen through a distorted lens. This often derives from a place of fear.

Empowering people is the key. Helping them fill their empty toolbox, their life toolbox. Some people don't even know they have a toolbox. That was where I started my journey. Or, as my good friend Bob has said, "I started on third base. *You* had to look for the field."

I have always had a curiosity for life and always wanted to know "why?" A girlfriend's nickname for me at age nineteen was "worm," as she always felt I asked deep-rooted questions. She was adopted and I remember being way more curious than she was about who gave birth to her, who was her biological father, does she have other siblings? She was too scared to find out.

She would say she didn't want to "open that can of worms" and I would be looking for the can opener. Daddy would often say, "You're better off with the devil you know than the devil you don't know." If I were told not to do something, I would be so curious about it I would do it and look for forgiveness afterward or pay the price.

As I got older, my good friend Jimmy nicknamed me "Dr. Phyllis," because when he started to talk or share information, I would observe him and hold him accountable for the situations he found himself in.

"OK, Dr. Phyllis," he'd say. We would laugh and then another deep question would come up, and he'd need to look inside himself for the answer instead of pointing the finger. It was like that adage, "When we are pointing the finger at someone, three are pointing back at ourselves."

The power lies in us, in our minds, in our knowing.

My work, and why I want to make a difference with people in the world—especially with women—comes in part from the work I did in Alcoholics Anonymous (AA) and other support groups, like Co-Dependents Anonymous (CoDA), individual and group therapy, and more.

The twelfth step in AA is having a spiritual awakening because of all the previous steps:

Step 12: "We tried to carry the message to other alcoholics and to practice these principles in all our affairs."

As a result of the years of therapy and life experiences I've had, I am now taking things a step further: I want to reach all the young—and not so young—ladies especially, who have not been heard, believed, or understood. The ones who still carry shame that never belonged to them in the first place.

The ones who are scared silent, like I was, for years.

The ones who feel alone in their distorted thoughts. The ones who have nightmares, the ones who don't want to be touched even by their loving partner, as their body is not able to differentiate between good and bad touch. The ones who lie awake in the middle of the night thinking they are completely alone. The ones who don't have an exact memory but know something happened.

° ° °

I'm still a work in progress.

The path I walk today includes exercising with my favorite trainer, Eric Miller, twice a week. I eat healthy foods most days and one of my favorite places to be is on my energy practitioner's table.

A Life Coach and Spiritual Consultant, Kristin Bredimus is a beautiful, bright light, a teacher, a healer and more. Her insights and knowledge, without judgement, are precious to me.

I also received one of the most beautiful messages this year from a wonderful soul, Jeanie Wesp, another spiritual consultant . Her exact words were, "You were born such a bright soul that darkness was attracted to you." I have never looked at things in this light before, but it resonated like it was my truth.

I remember another soul who once said I was my dad's bright star. I shared this with my person, Steve, recently and his exact reply was, "You're mine, as well. Sure, I had a hard time seeing through the darkness myself until you showed up. You're a light, and no mistake."

Our relationship, like all relationships, comes with luggage: his and mine. Our luggage was unzipped a few weeks in. Direct and honest dialogue is my wiring, so I confront issues as they arise. Not something Steve was used to.

I learned how to express myself freely and with respect, sometimes taking Steve off guard, and he would ask, "Where's this coming from?"

His first reaction would be to defend himself from my "attack." I learned how important holding space is when he is triggered, and I know that he usually needs a few hours or an overnight to process things.

As the months passed and our dialogue became easier, it took Steve less time to have a discussion. It seemed helpful to him when I was able to explain what was happening for me, how it affected me, and how it was not aimed at him personally, but rather the triggering of unhealed stuff.

I continue to do my best to talk to him with love, respect, and honesty. As he awakens, he is loving the journey: the journey to Self.

Our days continue to include travel, hikes, workouts, dinners, and movies. We have both decided recently to eat plant-based foods. Eating in has become a fun habit!

He sets the table with candles lit for dinner. Flowers await me every weekend, varying from hydrangea, to tulips, to roses. There are usually three vases arranged differently and set in the perfect places in his home.

The fire flickers in the background, the sunrises brighten the living room each morning, and the coffee aroma awakens Steve.

I still love my tea.

∘ ∘ ∘

All of this now becomes part of my story.

I came from abject poverty in Ireland, from abuse, alcoholism, addiction, and the prison of distorted thoughts that plagued my mind for many years. Today I live in the freedom of the United States of America and I have what I need: a warm, king-sized bed; more towels than I know what to do with; more shoes than days in a month (and no holes in them); and my own thriving business.

I feel I'm living in my purpose, with friends, a good relationship with many family members, and a love that I have never experienced before with a beautiful soul.

SPECIAL ACKNOWLEDGEMENTS

Dr. Mark Fanger, Ed.D., CST, CGP, without whom I would still be trapped in my own head and struggling to live. Mark held space for me every week in his office for many years, a place that became my 'home away from home', a place where I learned to grow up, and a safe place to unzip the secrets and the shame. Marks' non-judgement, strict boundaries, and his commitment to me and the work we had to do on a weekly basis, were the foundations I needed to finally move past the shame and to disarm myself on the field of battle between my own ears.

Dr. Neil Carter, Psychologist, PhD., without whom I would not have learned to manage the fears that my inner child was so scared of. Each week for about a year, we sat on the floor of his office, and he held me while I sobbed like a child. He helped me create a mental journey where we traveled back to Ireland in our minds, so I could reclaim Little Connie. That guided imagery was a helpful tool and a large part of my integration.

My parents, Mack and Mammy, they gave me life! I learned early on that they truly did their best, given the few tools they had in their toolbox. I'm grateful that I didn't have to hurt them with my unhealed 'brokenness'. I got to be a part of their last chapters and I did my best to make sure they weren't experiencing pain. [Thank You, to the Palliative Care team at Galway Hospice!]

And last, but by no means least, Steve DeWaters, my best friend, spiritual partner, lover, and My Person. I handed him what looked like the back of a tapestry, a tattered 'mess' frankly, in the form of random journal entries accumulated over many years. He somehow made sense of it all and was the guy behind the scenes, bringing this book to life. Thank you, thank you, thank you!

° ° °

I would also like to thank three individuals whose contributions were instructive and important along the way:

Laurie Chittenden, Freelance Content Development Editor

Ann Maynard, Owner and Lead Editor at Command+Z Content

Brooks Becker, Freelance Copy Editor